Plant-Based Air Fryer Cookbook for Beginners

1800 Days of Easy, Crispy, Delicious & Whole-Food
Recipes for Healthy Eating & Cooking Habits.
Includes 28-Day Meal Plan for Vegetarian & Vegan Lifestyle

Amanda Ray

© **Copyright 2025 - All rights reserved.**

The content contained within this book may not be reproduced, duplicated, or transmitted without direct written permission from the author or publisher.

Under no circumstances will any blame or legal responsibility be held against the publisher or author for any damages, reparations, or monetary losses due to the information contained within this book, either directly or indirectly.

Legal Notice:

This book is copyright-protected. It is only for personal use. You cannot amend, distribute, sell, use, quote, or paraphrase any part or the content within it without the consent of the author or publisher.

Disclaimer Notice:

Please note that the information contained within this document is for educational and entertainment purposes only. All efforts have been made to present accurate, up-to-date, reliable, and complete information. No warranties of any kind are declared or implied. Readers acknowledge that the author is not engaged in the rendering of legal, financial, medical, or professional advice. The content within this book has been derived from various sources. Please consult a licensed professional before attempting any techniques outlined in this book.

By reading this document, the reader agrees that under no circumstances is the author responsible for any losses, direct or indirect, that are incurred as a result of the use of the information contained within this document, including, but not limited to, errors, omissions, or inaccuracies.

Table of Content

Introduction 6

Chapter 1: Foundations of the Plant-Based Air Fryer Lifestyle 7
What Does It Mean to Eat Plant-Based? 7
Key Foods to Prioritize—and What to Skip 7
Smart Ingredient Swaps for Air Frying 9
Cooking Methods That Maximize Nutrition 10
Staying on Track Without Getting Bored 12

Chapter 2: Breakfasts 14
Sweet Potato Breakfast Boats 14
Air-Fried Banana Oat Patties 15
Chickpea Frittata Squares 15
Cinnamon-Spiced Quinoa Cakes 16
Zucchini-Lentil Breakfast Hash 16
Plantain and Black Bean Nuggets 17
Tofu-Turmeric Breakfast Cubes 17
Carrot Cake Baked Oat Squares 18
Apple-Cinnamon Breakfast Fries 18
Buckwheat & Date Mini Muffins 19
Avocado-Corn Breakfast Fritters 19
Mango Millet Breakfast Bites 20
Cauliflower-Potato Morning Tots 20
Air-Fried Berry Oat Clusters 21
Broccoli-Chickpea Mini Cakes 21
Crunchy Peanut Butter Oat Bites 22
Golden Lentil Breakfast Bars 22
Savory Oat and Mushroom Balls 23

Air-Fried Polenta Slices 23
Sweet Beet & Walnut Crisps 24
Parsnip & Leek Hash Cups 24
Quinoa-Pumpkin Mini Loaves 25
Green Pea and Herb Medallions 25
Coconut-Chia Breakfast Rolls 26
Spiced Butternut Breakfast Fries 26
Air-Fried Apple Buckwheat Slices 27
Tomato-Basil Breakfast Triangles 27
Millet-Cinnamon Crunch Wedges 28

Chapter 3: Snacks 29
Crispy Chickpea Snack Bombs 29
Air-Fried Carrot Zucchini Chips 30
Apple-Cinnamon Wedge Bites 30
Curried Lentil Poppers 31
Sweet Potato Toast Fingers 31
Seasoned Green Pea Crunch 32
Roasted Cauliflower Nuggets 32
Corn & Black Bean Snack Balls 33
Crunchy Quinoa Clusters 33
Parsnip & Herb Wedges 34
Plantain & Walnut Munchies 34
Tofu-Celery Air Sticks 35
Sweet Date-Coconut Balls 35
Spicy Mushroom Snack Cubes 36
Lemon-Garlic Broccoli Bites 36
Beet Hummus Air-Fry Chips 37
Ginger-Oat Mini Discs 37
Pumpkin-Crisp Snack Cakes 38
Maple Carrot Oat Crunch 38
Seaweed & Rice Crumble Squares 39
Crunchy Cucumber Tofu Rolls 39
Spiced Lentil Bites with Dill 40

Banana-Almond Air Coins 40
Avocado & Quinoa Wafers 41
Chickpea-Cranberry Crisps 41
Jicama Lime Snack Cubes 42
Curry-Spiced Sweet Potato Slices 42
Roasted Garlic Cauliflower Florets 43

Chapter 4: Lunches 44
Curried Chickpea Air Logs 44
Air-Fried Falafel Wrap 45
Roasted Veggie Stuffed Pita 45
Lentil & Brown Rice Patties 46
Thai-Inspired Tofu Lettuce Boats 46
Air-Fried Mushroom-Spinach Rolls 47
Sweet Potato Chickpea Pockets 47
Crispy Quinoa Salad Bites 48
Zucchini-Carrot Fritter Sandwich 48
Eggplant-Bulgur Medallions 49
Tofu Kale Crunch Wrap 49
Smoky Black Bean Air Cakes 50
Roasted Red Pepper & Hummus Wrap 50
Tomato-Lentil Crunch Sliders 51
Chickpea-Cauliflower Air Balls 51
Broccoli-Sweet Potato Pocket 52
Millet-Lime Veggie Boats 52
Crunchy Parsnip Wraps 53
Carrot-Lentil Air Burgers 53
Cucumber Quinoa Salad Wrap 54
Spicy Edamame Lettuce Cups 54
Green Bean & Rice Cakes 55
Herbed Zucchini Tofu Discs 55
BBQ Cauliflower Pita Pockets 56
Garlic Sweet Corn Cakes 56
Air-Fried Tempeh Veggie Skewers 57
Roasted Root Veggie Samosas 57
Mushroom Brown Rice Nori Wraps 58

Chapter 5: Dinners 59
Cauliflower-Lentil Kofta 59
Air-Fried Tofu Steak with Chimichurri.. 60
Spaghetti Squash Veggie Balls 60
Butternut Chickpea Hash Stack 61
Eggplant-Millet Air Parm 61
Moroccan-Spiced Carrot Patties 62
Sweet Potato & Kale Air Casserole 62
Zucchini Lentil Lasagna Cups 63
Crunchy Quinoa-Stuffed Peppers 63
Broccoli-Cauliflower Curry Bites 64

Curried Rice and Chickpea
Cakes 64
Tofu-Pumpkin Rice Bake 65
Mushroom-Stuffed Polenta
Squares 65
Roasted Brussels Veggie Mix 66
Cabbage-Wrapped Spiced Lentils 66
Air-Fried Gnocchi with Herbs 67
Crispy Eggplant and Corn Patties 67
Chickpea Mushroom
Stroganoff Bites 68
Carrot-Zucchini Noodle Balls 68
Crunchy Black Bean Tofu Steaks 69
Creamy Spinach Quinoa Cups 69
Air-Fried Vegetable Tikka Parcels 70
Sweet Corn & Leek Galettes 70
Baked Turmeric Cauliflower Slabs 71
Lentil-Rice Patties with
Avocado Drizzle 71
Tofu Stuffed Portobello Caps 72
Roasted Pepper Rice Cakes 72
Pumpkin-Spinach Air-Fry
Casserole 73

Chapter 6: Desserts 74
Air-Fried Date-Nut Bars 74
Crispy Banana Oat Crumble 75
Sweet Apple Lentil Muffins 75
Chocolate Chickpea Crunch Bites 76
Baked Cinnamon Quinoa Squares 76
Coconut-Carrot Pudding Cups 77
Peanut Butter Apple Wedges 77
Air-Fried Berry-Filled Oat Discs 78
Roasted Pear and Almond Rounds 78
Pumpkin-Chia Spice Cookies 79
Maple-Glazed Sweet Potato Coins 79
Mango Coconut Rice Puffs 80
Banana-Cocoa Mini Cakes 80
Orange-Date Bliss Squares 81
Air-Fried Almond-Cinnamon
Twists 81
Apricot-Oat Tartlets 82
Stuffed Baked Figs with Walnuts 82
Apple-Raisin Oat Rounds 83
Ginger Beet Cookie Slices 83
Vanilla Millet Pudding Puffs 84
Cinnamon-Roasted Carrot Bars 84
Tahini-Date Energy Donuts 85

Chocolate Avocado Truffle Balls............85
Peach-Buckwheat Crisp 86
Air-Fried Polenta Lemon Wedges........86
Pineapple Basil Dessert Skewers 87
Roasted Strawberry Oat Fritters............87
Blueberry-Lime Crisp Cubes 88

Chapter 7: 28-Day Meal Prep Plan 89
Week 1: 89
Week 2: 89
Week 3: 90
Week 4: 90

Free Gift.. 91

Conclusion outline............................92

References 93

Appendix 1: Measurement Conversion Chart 94

Appendix 2: Index Recipes 95
A 95
B 95
C 95
D 96
E 96
F..96
G 96
J...96
L 296
M 96
O 96
P..97
Q 97
R 97
S..97
T..97
V 98
W 98
Z..98

Notes...99

Introduction

If you're curious about plant-based eating but unsure where to start—or if you're already on the journey and looking to make it even easier—this cookbook is for you. The Plant-Based Air Fryer Cookbook for Beginners brings together two of the most powerful wellness trends in one place: whole-food, plant-based eating and the convenience of air frying. Whether you want to feel more energized, improve heart health, support the planet, or simply enjoy delicious food, this book will help you cook smarter, not harder. Eating a plant-based diet means focusing on foods that come from plants: vegetables, fruits, whole grains, legumes, nuts, seeds, and healthy oils. It's a lifestyle that prioritizes nutrients, fiber, and antioxidants while naturally minimizing saturated fats, cholesterol, and ultra-processed ingredients. And no, it doesn't mean eating bland salads or giving up your favorite comfort foods. In fact, with the help of the air fryer, you can enjoy crispy tofu bites, golden potato wedges, crunchy veggie fritters, and even warm desserts—all with a fraction of the oil and time you'd need in traditional cooking methods.

Air fryers have revolutionized healthy home cooking. They use hot air circulation to create the crispy textures we love, without deep frying. That means fewer calories and less fat, but still a big flavor and satisfying crunch. The air fryer is a game-changer for beginners—easy to use, quick to clean, and perfect for making single or double servings without heating the whole kitchen.

This cookbook is designed specifically for beginners. You'll find easy-to-follow, 100% plant-based recipes made with simple ingredients you can find at any grocery store. Each recipe takes 30 minutes or less, focuses on whole foods, and avoids refined sugars, processed oils, and artificial ingredients. You'll also get tips on how to use your air fryer efficiently, build a balanced plant-based plate, and adapt recipes to suit your personal taste or dietary needs.

Whether you're looking to improve your health, support animal welfare, reduce your environmental footprint, or just explore a delicious new way of eating, this book's recipes inspire you. So plug in your air fryer, grab a handful of fresh veggies, and let's get started cooking!

Chapter 1: Foundations of the Plant-Based Air Fryer Lifestyle

What Does It Mean to Eat Plant-Based?

Let's start at the beginning—what exactly does it mean to eat plant-based? You've probably heard the term thrown around in health magazines, social media posts, and maybe even at your local grocery store. But "plant-based" isn't just a trend. It's a way of eating that puts real, whole foods from plants at the center of your plate.

A plant-based diet is centered around vegetables, fruits, whole grains, legumes (like beans, lentils, and peas), nuts, and seeds. These foods are packed with fiber, vitamins, minerals, and antioxidants that support your body in every way—from digestion and immunity to heart health and energy levels. And when we say "whole," we mean foods that are as close to their natural state as possible. Think roasted sweet potatoes, quinoa, steamed broccoli, or a handful of almonds—not heavily processed snacks with long ingredient lists.

A plant-based diet focuses on inclusion rather than strict exclusion. It's not necessarily about being 100% vegan or vegetarian (though it can be). It's about choosing plant foods more often and minimizing animal products, processed foods, added sugars, and refined oils. That's what makes this lifestyle flexible and approachable, especially for beginners.

So, how is it different from veganism? A vegan diet eliminates all animal products, including meat, dairy, eggs, and even honey. While veganism often comes from an ethical standpoint, being plant-based is more about health and wellness. It doesn't always mean eliminating all animal products, but rather reducing them significantly and focusing on nutrient-dense, plant-powered meals. For many people, this feels more sustainable and less overwhelming.

Why go plant-based? The health benefits are wide-ranging and well-supported by research. A diet rich in whole plant foods can help lower blood pressure, reduce cholesterol levels, support a healthy weight, lower the risk of type 2 diabetes, and even reduce inflammation in the body. It's also good for the planet—plant-based diets use fewer natural resources and create less pollution than meat-heavy ones.

And here's the best part: plant-based eating can be delicious and deeply satisfying. With the help of the air fryer, you can enjoy crispy tofu, roasted vegetables, sweet potato fries, and more—all with less oil and in less time. You're not giving up flavor or comfort—just cooking smarter.

This cookbook guides you to building a simple, joyful, and nourishing plant-based routine. You'll discover how easy it is to turn everyday veggies and grains into crave-worthy dishes—and how to stock your kitchen so that you're always ready to create something wholesome.

So, if you're wondering whether plant-based eating is for you, the answer is yes, it can be. Whether you're ready to go all-in or just want to start with a few meals a week, every plant-powered choice makes a difference. The goal isn't perfection—it's progress.

Key Foods to Prioritize—and What to Skip

One of the best things about plant-based air fryer cooking is how simple and nourishing it can be, once you stock your kitchen with the right ingredients. In this chapter, we'll walk through the key foods to prioritize for everyday cooking and which ones to skip so you can make healthy meals that taste great and support your long-term wellness goals.

What to Prioritize

When building your plant-based pantry, think *wholesome, minimally processed, and full of natural flavor.* Here's what that looks like:

1. **Fresh and Frozen Vegetables**

Vegetables are the heart of any plant-based diet, and your air fryer makes them crisp, flavorful, and satisfying. Stock up on a variety:

- **Fresh staples:** broccoli, cauliflower, carrots, bell peppers, zucchini, mushrooms, and sweet potatoes
- **Frozen go-tos:** green beans, Brussels sprouts, corn, peas, and spinach
  Frozen vegetables are great for quick meals and retain their nutrients for a more extended period.

2. **Whole Grains**

Grains like brown rice, quinoa, farro, oats, and millet are excellent sources of fiber, energy, and essential nutrients.

Tip: Cook a batch of grains ahead of time and use your air fryer to crisp them into grain cakes or warm bowls.

3. **Legumes**

Beans, lentils, and peas are rich in protein and super versatile. Chickpeas, black beans, lentils, and edamame are great air fryer-friendly options. Roasted chickpeas, for example, make a crunchy snack or salad topper.

4. **Nuts and Seeds**

Almonds, walnuts, flaxseeds, chia seeds, sunflower seeds, and hemp hearts are rich in healthy fats, protein, and fiber. Use them to add texture or make homemade air-fried granola.

5. **Healthy Fats**
   - Instead of processed oils, go for:
   - **Avocado or tahini as** a creamy base
   - **Nut butters** (like almond or cashew) for sauces and dressings
   - **Olives and nuts** for richness and crunch
     Use a small amount of extra virgin olive oil, if needed, in spray form for even air fryer coating.

6. **Herbs, Spices, and Natural Flavor Enhancers**

Keep your meals exciting with dried herbs (like thyme, rosemary, oregano), spices (paprika, turmeric, cumin), and flavor boosters like:

- Nutritional yeast (cheesy flavor without dairy)
- Fresh garlic and ginger
- Citrus zest and juice
- Apple cider vinegar or balsamic vinegar
- Low-sodium tamari or coconut aminos

What to Skip

While the grocery store is filled with "plant-based" products, not all of them are healthy. Here's what to watch out for:

1. Processed Meat Substitutes

Many vegan burgers, sausages, and "chicken" nuggets are heavily processed, high in sodium, and loaded with additives. They may be plant-based, but they're far from whole food. Instead, use lentils, beans, mushrooms, or tofu as your protein base.

2. Hydrogenated and Refined Oils

These oils—such as corn oil, vegetable shortening, and margarine—are highly processed and stripped of nutrients. They can also contribute to inflammation. Use whole-food fat sources instead.

3. Added Sugars

Watch out for cane sugar, corn syrup, and even some "natural" sweeteners in sauces, dressings, and packaged foods. Choose fresh fruit, date syrup, or maple syrup in small amounts to add sweetness naturally.

4. Excess Sodium

Many store-bought sauces, canned foods, and meat substitutes contain high levels of sodium. Look for low-sodium versions, rinse canned beans before using, and use herbs and spices for flavor instead of salt.

5. White Flour and Refined Grains

These include white bread, white pasta, and baked goods made with refined flour. Choose whole-grain versions whenever possible for more fiber and sustained energy.

Smart Ingredient Swaps for Air Frying

Air fryers are a game-changer for anyone looking to eat healthier without giving up crunch and flavor. When you pair air frying with a plant-based lifestyle, you get the best of both worlds: delicious meals made with wholesome ingredients, minus the heavy oils and animal products. However, to truly maximize the benefits of your air fryer, it's essential to learn how to make informed ingredient swaps. These swaps help you achieve that golden-brown, crisp, and rich taste.

Let's break down how to rethink traditional air-fried recipes and turn them into plant-based, oil-free (or low-oil) delights.

1. Use Whole-Grain Breadcrumbs Instead of White

Breadcrumbs are another ingredient that can make or break the crunch factor. The classic kind is often made with white flour and sometimes includes dairy. Instead, opt for whole-grain or sprouted-grain breadcrumbs. These are higher in fiber, better for blood sugar levels, and just as crispy.

Even better? Make your own! Toast whole-grain bread until dry, then pulse it in a blender or food processor until it reaches a fine texture.

You can also try:

- **Rolled oats,** lightly ground
- **Crushed whole-grain crackers or rice cakes**
- **Cornmeal,** for extra crunch with a Southern-style twist

2. Add Nutritional Yeast for Flavor and Texture

Nutritional yeast isn't just for cheesy flavor—it's also a smart way to add extra crispness and nutrition to your coatings. It's rich in B vitamins and has a savory, umami taste that elevates anything you sprinkle it on.

Try this combo for coating:

- 1/2 cup whole-grain breadcrumbs
- 2 tbsp nutritional yeast
- 1 tsp garlic powder
- 1/2 tsp smoked paprika

Toss tofu cubes or veggie slices in this mix. Air fry until crispy—pure plant-based magic.

3. Make Smart Flour Swaps

Need a batter or a dredge? Regular flour can be replaced with more nutritious alternatives:

- **Chickpea flour:** High in protein and makes a great binder.
- **Brown rice flour:** Lighter and slightly crispy when cooked.
- **Oat flour:** Naturally gluten-free and fiber-rich.
- **Whole-wheat flour:** For more fiber and a nutty flavor.

Mix your flour with herbs and spices to amp up the flavor. You can even add a little baking powder for extra puffiness in batters.

4. Use Plant-Based Binders

To help coatings stick without the need for eggs or aquafaba, here are some easy plant-based binders you can use:

- **Unsweetened plant milk (soy, almond, oat, etc.):** Great for light coatings and keeping things simple.
- **Flax or chia "egg" (1 tbsp ground flax or chia seeds + 2.5 tbsp water):** Perfect for heavier coatings or where extra binding is needed.
- **Cornstarch or arrowroot slurry (1–2 tbsp starch + 2–3 tbsp water):** Creates a crisp, light finish and works well for delicate items.
- **Mustard (thinned with a bit of water or plant milk):** Adds tangy flavor and stickiness—excellent for savory recipes.

Cooking Methods That Maximize Nutrition

When it comes to cooking plant-based meals, one of the primary goals is retaining the nutrients that make these foods so beneficial for us. Air frying is already a great head start—it uses less (or no) oil, cooks faster than an oven, and keeps food crispy without deep frying. However, to get the most nutrition from your food, it helps to understand the process behind cooking.

1. Dry Roasting for Flavor and Nutrient Retention

Dry roasting is one of the easiest and healthiest methods for using an air fryer. It's exactly what it sounds like—cooking food without oil or water. When you roast veggies or nuts in the air fryer this way, you concentrate their flavors while minimizing nutrient loss that can occur from boiling or deep-frying.

Great for:

- Broccoli florets
- Carrot sticks
- Cauliflower bites
- Chickpeas
- Nuts and seeds

Tips for success:
- Preheat your air fryer so the food crisps evenly from the start.
- Use smaller, evenly cut pieces for consistent cooking.
- Shake the basket halfway through to avoid burning on one side.

2. Air Steaming with Water-Rich Veggies

Surprisingly, your air fryer can mimic a gentle steaming effect, without needing a pot of boiling water. When you cook water-rich vegetables (like zucchini, mushrooms, or bell peppers), their moisture naturally steams them from the inside out. The trick is not overloading the basket and cooking at a lower temperature.

Best vegetables for this:
- Zucchini
- Eggplant
- Mushrooms
- Bell peppers
- Summer squash

Technique:
- Slice vegetables evenly and avoid overcrowding.
- Cook at 160–175°C [320–350°F] for a shorter time (8–12 minutes).
- Shake once or twice to ensure even texture.

3. Timing Tricks for Plant-Based Proteins

Plant-based proteins—such as tofu, tempeh, or seitan—can become rubbery or dry if cooked for too long. Getting the timing right is key to keeping them tender on the inside and lightly crisp on the outside.

Here's how to make them shine:
- **Tofu:** Press it first to remove excess water, then cube it. Air fry at 190°C [375°F] for 12–15 minutes. Marinate beforehand for extra flavor.
- **Tempeh:** Steam it first if it tastes too bitter. Slice and cook at 180°C [360°F] for 10–12 minutes.
- **Seitan:** Best air-fried in thin strips, 200°C [390°F] for just 8–10 minutes. Brush with a bit of low-sodium sauce or tamari if needed.

Shorter cook times and careful spacing in the basket prevent overcooking, helping to preserve protein structure and key minerals like iron and zinc.

4. Layering Ingredients for Balanced Texture

When air-frying meals with multiple components, such as tofu and veggies together, timing is crucial. Some foods require more time, while others require less. Instead of dumping everything in at once, cook in layers or stagger your additions.

Example:
- Start with harder veggies like sweet potato or carrots.
- Halfway through, add softer veggies like zucchini or mushrooms.
- Add tofu or tempeh cubes near the end to keep them moist but crispy.

This approach ensures that everything is cooked just right and prevents nutrient loss from overcooking delicate items.

5. Use Lower Heat When Possible

Higher heat can lead to faster cooking, but it may also destroy certain heat-sensitive nutrients, like vitamin C, some antioxidants, and folate. When your goal is maximum nutrition, a moderate temperature is your friend.

Guidelines:
- Leafy greens: 150–160°C [300–320°F]
- Soft veggies: 160–175°C [320–350°F]
- Root veggies and legumes: 180–200°C [355–390°F]

You can always finish with a quick blast of higher heat at the end for crunch, but a slower start helps lock in the good stuff.

Staying on Track Without Getting Bored

One of the biggest challenges when following a plant-based lifestyle, especially with a specific tool like an air fryer, is keeping meals exciting. It's easy to fall into a rut of repeating the same dishes, such as crispy tofu or roasted sweet potatoes, every week. And while those are delicious, variety is what keeps your taste buds happy and your motivation strong.

The good news? With a few simple strategies, you can keep things fresh, flavorful, and easy, without spending hours in the kitchen or buying a cart full of ingredients. This chapter guides you through building variety into your plant-based air fryer meals while staying on track with your health goals.

1. Batch Prep Smart, Not Just Big

Meal prepping doesn't mean cooking entire meals days in advance. It can be as simple as prepping versatile components you can mix and match throughout the week.

Use your air fryer to batch-cook:
- **Chickpeas:** Roast with different seasonings (paprika, garlic, cumin, or even cinnamon) for a protein-packed snack or salad topper.
- **Tofu or tempeh:** Air fry in cubes or strips and store for quick lunch bowls or wraps.
- **Veggies:** Roast batches of carrots, bell peppers, cauliflower, or zucchini—ready to add to grain bowls, tacos, or soups.

Once these components are cooked, store them separately in airtight containers. During the week, just grab, mix, and enjoy. You get endless variety from just a few base ingredients.

2. Rotate Flavor Profiles with Herbs and Spices

Seasoning is everything when it comes to making plant-based meals exciting. Without meat or dairy, your flavors come from spices, herbs, sauces, and textures. The air fryer enhances the aroma of spices during cooking, bringing out their flavor and adding depth to the dish.

Try rotating flavor themes each week:
- **Mediterranean:** Garlic, oregano, lemon zest, smoked paprika
- **Asian-inspired:** Ginger, soy sauce (or tamari), sesame seeds, scallions
- **Latin-style:** Cumin, lime, chili powder, cilantro
- **Indian:** Turmeric, coriander, curry powder, garam masala

Keep a rotating list on your fridge or pantry door. That way, even if you're eating the same main ingredient (like tofu or chickpeas), the flavor will feel completely new depending on the seasoning.

3. Make the Most of Air-Fried Snacks

Snacks can be both fun and nourishing when you have an air fryer. They're also a great way to keep things interesting between meals, without relying on store-bought, ultra-processed foods.

Quick and satisfying air fryer snacks:
- **Stuffed mini bell peppers** with hummus or lentil spread
- **Crispy kale chips** tossed with lemon juice and nutritional yeast
- **Sweet potato fries** with cinnamon or chili-lime seasoning
- **Apple slices** sprinkled with cinnamon and air-fried until soft and warm
- **Roasted edamame** with garlic powder and a pinch of salt-free spice blend

These take 10–15 minutes at most and offer different flavors and textures that keep you from reaching for less nutritious choices.

4. Switch Up Your Cooking Method—Even in the Air Fryer

Believe it or not, your air fryer can do more than just "fry." Depending on temperature and timing, you can:
- **Bake** small muffins, energy bites, or veggie patties using silicone molds
- **Roast** dense veggies like beets or sweet potatoes until naturally caramelized
- **Toast** nuts and seeds for granolas or salads
- **Reheat** leftovers without drying them out
- **Dehydrate** fruit slices for chewy, no-added-sugar snacks

Changing how you use the air fryer gives your meals a whole new feel, even if the ingredients stay the same.

5. Build Mix-and-Match Bowls and Wraps

Bowls and wraps are lifesavers when it comes to building variety with ease. Once you've batch-cooked your staples and prepared a few fresh items, just assemble in different ways.

A balanced bowl formula:
- A base (quinoa, brown rice, or greens)
- A protein (tofu, tempeh, lentils, chickpeas)
- Roasted veggies (from your air fryer batch prep)
- A sauce or dressing (tahini, salsa, avocado mash)
- Crunchy toppings (nuts, seeds, air-fried chickpeas)

CHAPTER 1: FOUNDATIONS OF THE PLANT-BASED AIR FRYER LIFESTYLE

Chapter 2: Breakfasts

Sweet Potato Breakfast Boats

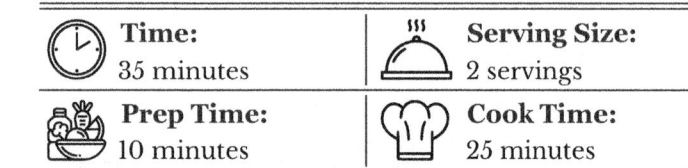

Time: 35 minutes	Serving Size: 2 servings
Prep Time: 10 minutes	Cook Time: 25 minutes

Each Serving Has:
Calories: 280, Carbohydrates: 47g, Saturated Fat: 0.6g, Protein: 6g, Fat: 7g, Sodium: 90mg, Potassium: 630mg, Fiber: 7g, Sugar: 9g, Vitamin C: 18mg, Calcium: 50mg, Iron: 1.9mg

Ingredients:
- 1 medium [250g] sweet potato, halved lengthwise
- 1/2 cup [85g] cooked and rinsed black beans
- 1/4 cup [30g] diced red bell pepper
- 1/4 cup [30g] diced red onion
- 1 tbsp chopped fresh cilantro
- 1/2 tsp ground cumin
- 1/4 tsp smoked paprika

Directions:
1. Preheat the air fryer to 375°F [190°C].
2. Place the halved sweet potato in the air fryer basket, cut-side down.
3. Cook for 20 minutes, or until the sweet potato is tender when pierced with a fork.
4. While the sweet potato cooks, combine the cooked black beans, diced bell pepper, onion, chopped cilantro, cumin, and smoked paprika in a mixing bowl. Toss gently to mix the ingredients evenly.
5. Remove the sweet potato halves from the air fryer and carefully scoop out a small amount from the center of each to create a shallow "boat." Mash the scooped-out portion into the filling.
6. Fill each sweet potato half with the bean and veggie mixture, gently pressing to pack it in.
7. Return the filled sweet potatoes to the air fryer basket and cook for an additional 5 minutes to heat through.
8. Remove the boats from the air fryer and serve.

Air-Fried Banana Oat Patties

⏲ Time: 25 minutes	🍽 Serving Size: 2 servings
🥗 Prep Time: 10 minutes	👨‍🍳 Cook Time: 15 minutes

Each Serving Has:
Calories: 210, Carbohydrates: 38g, Saturated Fat: 0.4g, Protein: 5g, Fat: 4g, Sodium: 60mg, Potassium: 360mg, Fiber: 5g, Sugar: 10g, Vitamin C: 4mg, Calcium: 30mg, Iron: 1.6mg

Ingredients:
- 1 medium [120g] mashed ripe banana
- 1/2 cup [45g] rolled oats
- 2 tbsp chopped raw walnuts
- 1 tbsp ground flaxseed
- 1/2 tsp ground cinnamon
- 1/4 tsp vanilla extract
- 1/8 tsp sea salt

Directions:
1. Preheat the air fryer to 350°F [175°C].
2. In a medium bowl, combine the mashed banana, oats, ground flaxseed, cinnamon, vanilla extract, and sea salt. Mix until a sticky, uniform dough forms.
3. Fold in the chopped walnuts, ensuring they are evenly distributed throughout the mixture.
4. Divide the mixture into two equal portions and shape into round, slightly flattened patties about 3 inches [7.5 cm] wide.
5. Place the patties in the air fryer basket, leaving space between them for even cooking.
6. Cook for 15 minutes, flipping the patties once halfway through, until the edges are golden and they feel firm to the touch.
7. Let the patties cool for 2–3 minutes before serving.

Chickpea Frittata Squares

⏲ Time: 30 minutes	🍽 Serving Size: 2 servings
🥗 Prep Time: 10 minutes	👨‍🍳 Cook Time: 20 minutes

Each Serving Has:
Calories: 245, Carbohydrates: 30g, Saturated Fat: 0.5g, Protein: 11g, Fat: 7g, Sodium: 310mg, Potassium: 510mg, Fiber: 7g, Sugar: 4g, Vitamin C: 19mg, Calcium: 45mg, Iron: 2.4mg

Ingredients:
- 1/2 cup [60g] chickpea flour
- 1/2 cup [120ml] water
- 1/4 cup [40g] diced red bell pepper
- 1/4 cup [40g] chopped zucchini
- 1/4 cup [40g] chopped red onion
- 2 tbsp chopped fresh parsley
- 1/4 tsp ground turmeric
- 1/4 tsp garlic powder
- 1/4 tsp sea salt
- 1/8 tsp black pepper

Directions:
1. Preheat the air fryer to 350°F [175°C].
2. In a mixing bowl, whisk the chickpea flour and water until smooth and lump-free.
3. Stir in the diced bell pepper, chopped zucchini, onion, parsley, turmeric, garlic powder, sea salt, and black pepper. Mix until all ingredients are evenly combined.
4. Pour the mixture into a small square silicone or oven-safe baking dish that fits in your air fryer basket, spreading it into an even layer.
5. Place the dish in the air fryer and cook for 20 minutes, or until the center is firm and the edges are golden.
6. Let it cool slightly before slicing into squares.

Cinnamon-Spiced Quinoa Cakes

🕐	**Time:** 30 minutes	🍽	**Serving Size:** 2 servings
🥗	**Prep Time:** 10 minutes	👨‍🍳	**Cook Time:** 20 minutes

Each Serving Has:
Calories: 230, Carbohydrates: 34g, Saturated Fat: 0.6g, Protein: 6g, Fat: 6g, Sodium: 95mg, Potassium: 290mg, Fiber: 5g, Sugar: 4g, Vitamin C: 1mg, Calcium: 40mg, Iron: 2.1mg

Ingredients:
- 1/2 cup [90g] cooked and cooled quinoa
- 1/4 cup [60g] mashed ripe banana
- 2 tbsp grated carrot
- 2 tbsp chopped raw walnuts
- 1 tbsp ground flaxseed
- 1/2 tsp ground cinnamon
- 1/8 tsp ground nutmeg

Directions:
1. Preheat the air fryer to 350°F [175°C].
2. In a medium bowl, combine the cooked quinoa, mashed banana, grated carrot, chopped walnuts, ground flaxseed, cinnamon, and nutmeg. Mix thoroughly until a sticky, uniform mixture forms.
3. Divide the mixture in half and shape into two round, compact cakes about 1 inch [2.5 cm] thick.
4. Place the quinoa cakes in the air fryer basket, leaving space between them.
5. Cook for 20 minutes, flipping gently halfway through, until the edges are golden and the cakes are firm to the touch.
6. Let the cakes cool slightly before serving.

Zucchini-Lentil Breakfast Hash

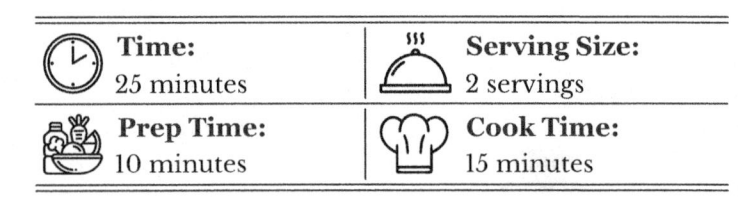

🕐	**Time:** 25 minutes	🍽	**Serving Size:** 2 servings
🥗	**Prep Time:** 10 minutes	👨‍🍳	**Cook Time:** 15 minutes

Each Serving Has:
Calories: 230, Carbohydrates: 30g, Saturated Fat: 0.4g, Protein: 12g, Fat: 5g, Sodium: 180mg, Potassium: 660mg, Fiber: 9g, Sugar: 5g, Vitamin C: 22mg, Calcium: 45mg, Iron: 3.2mg

Ingredients:
- 1 cup [150g] diced zucchini
- 1/2 cup [80g] chopped red bell pepper
- 1/2 cup [80g] chopped red onion
- 3/4 cup [120g] cooked green or brown lentils, drained
- 1 tbsp chopped fresh parsley
- 1 tbsp olive oil
- 1/2 tsp garlic powder
- 1/2 tsp ground cumin
- 1/4 tsp sea salt
- 1/8 tsp black pepper

Directions:
1. Preheat the air fryer to 375°F [190°C].
2. In a mixing bowl, toss the diced zucchini, chopped bell pepper, onion, and cooked lentils with olive oil, garlic powder, cumin, sea salt, and black pepper until evenly coated.
3. Transfer the mixture to the air fryer basket and spread it evenly in a layer.
4. Cook for 15 minutes, shaking the basket halfway through to promote even browning.
5. Sprinkle with the chopped parsley before serving.

Plantain and Black Bean Nuggets

Time: 30 minutes	Serving Size: 2 servings
Prep Time: 10 minutes	Cook Time: 20 minutes

Each Serving Has:
Calories: 260, Carbohydrates: 41g, Saturated Fat: 0.6g, Protein: 8g, Fat: 6g, Sodium: 150mg, Potassium: 620mg, Fiber: 9g, Sugar: 12g, Vitamin C: 17mg, Calcium: 35mg, Iron: 2.6mg

Ingredients:
- 1/2 cup [110g] mashed ripe plantain
- 1/2 cup [85g] cooked black beans, rinsed and drained
- 1/4 cup [40g] chopped red bell pepper
- 1/4 cup [30g] chopped red onion
- 1 tbsp ground flaxseed
- 2 tbsp rolled oats
- 1/2 tsp ground cumin
- 1/4 tsp smoked paprika
- 1/8 tsp black pepper
- 1 tbsp olive oil

Directions:
1. Preheat the air fryer to 375°F [190°C].
2. In a medium bowl, combine the mashed plantain, cooked black beans, chopped bell pepper, onion, ground flaxseed, oats, cumin, smoked paprika, and black pepper. Mash and mix until the mixture holds together but still has some texture.
3. Form the mixture into 6 nugget-shaped patties, pressing firmly to ensure they hold their shape.
4. Brush the nuggets lightly with olive oil on all sides.
5. Arrange the nuggets in a single layer in the air fryer basket.
6. Cook for 20 minutes, flipping halfway through, until golden brown and slightly crisp on the edges.
7. Remove the nuggets from the air fryer and serve.

Tofu-Turmeric Breakfast Cubes

Time: 25 minutes	Serving Size: 2 servings
Prep Time: 10 minutes	Cook Time: 15 minutes

Each Serving Has:
Calories: 210, Carbohydrates: 7g, Saturated Fat: 0.7g, Protein: 19g, Fat: 12g, Sodium: 310mg, Potassium: 320mg, Fiber: 2g, Sugar: 2g, Vitamin C: 6mg, Calcium: 280mg, Iron: 3.1mg

Ingredients:
- 1 block [200g] firm tofu, pressed and cubed
- 1/2 cup [75g] chopped red bell pepper
- 1/4 cup [40g] chopped red onion
- 1 tbsp olive oil
- 1/2 tsp ground turmeric
- 1/2 tsp garlic powder
- 1/4 tsp ground cumin
- 1/4 tsp sea salt
- 1/8 tsp black pepper

Directions:
1. Preheat the air fryer to 375°F [190°C].
2. In a bowl, toss the cubed firm tofu, chopped bell pepper, and onion with olive oil, turmeric, garlic powder, cumin, sea salt, and black pepper until evenly coated.
3. Arrange the tofu mixture in a single layer in the air fryer basket.
4. Cook for 15 minutes, shaking the basket halfway through to ensure even browning.
5. Remove the cubes from the air fryer and serve.

Carrot Cake Baked Oat Squares

⏱ Time: 30 minutes	🍽 Serving Size: 2 servings
🥗 Prep Time: 10 minutes	👨‍🍳 Cook Time: 20 minutes

Each Serving Has:
Calories: 240, Carbohydrates: 36g, Saturated Fat: 0.8g, Protein: 6g, Fat: 8g, Sodium: 115mg, Potassium: 370mg, Fiber: 5g, Sugar: 8g, Vitamin C: 1mg, Calcium: 45mg, Iron: 2mg

Ingredients:
- 1/2 cup [45g] rolled oats
- 1/2 cup [120ml] unsweetened almond milk
- 1/4 cup [30g] grated carrot
- 1/4 cup [60g] mashed ripe banana
- 2 tbsp chopped raw walnuts
- 1 tbsp ground flaxseed
- 1/2 tsp ground cinnamon
- 1/4 tsp ground ginger
- 1/4 tsp baking powder
- 1/8 tsp sea salt

Directions:
1. Preheat the air fryer to 350°F [175°C].
2. In a medium bowl, combine the oats, almond milk, mashed banana, grated carrot, chopped walnuts, ground flaxseed, cinnamon, ginger, baking powder, and sea salt. Stir until the mixture is well incorporated and thick.
3. Pour the mixture into a small silicone or oven-safe baking dish that fits into your air fryer basket. Spread evenly into a square or rectangle about 1 inch [2.5 cm] thick.
4. Place the dish in the air fryer and cook for 20 minutes, or until the top is golden and firm to the touch.
5. Let it cool slightly before slicing into squares.

Apple-Cinnamon Breakfast Fries

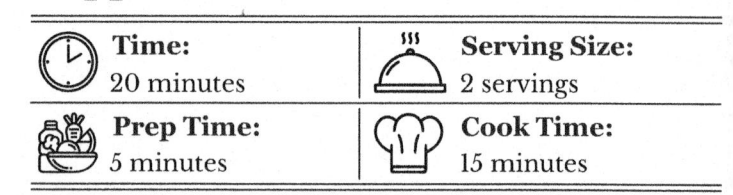

⏱ Time: 20 minutes	🍽 Serving Size: 2 servings
🥗 Prep Time: 5 minutes	👨‍🍳 Cook Time: 15 minutes

Each Serving Has:
Calories: 170, Carbohydrates: 38g, Saturated Fat: 0.4g, Protein: 1g, Fat: 2g, Sodium: 0mg, Potassium: 260mg, Fiber: 5g, Sugar: 25g, Vitamin C: 10mg, Calcium: 15mg, Iron: 0.4mg

Ingredients:
- 2 medium [300g] crisp apples, peeled and cut into thin fry-shaped sticks
- 1 tsp olive oil
- 1/2 tsp ground cinnamon
- 1/4 tsp ground ginger
- 1 tbsp ground flaxseed

Directions:
1. Preheat the air fryer to 375°F [190°C].
2. In a bowl, toss the apple sticks with olive oil, cinnamon, ginger, and ground flaxseed until the sticks are evenly coated.
3. Arrange the apple sticks in a single layer in the air fryer basket, spacing them slightly apart for even crisping.
4. Cook for 15 minutes, shaking the basket gently halfway through to promote uniform browning.
5. Let the fries cool slightly before serving them warm.

Buckwheat & Date Mini Muffins

Time: 25 minutes
Serving Size: 2 servings
Prep Time: 10 minutes
Cook Time: 15 minutes

Each Serving Has:
Calories: 220, Carbohydrates: 37g, Saturated Fat: 0.6g, Protein: 5g, Fat: 6g, Sodium: 90mg, Potassium: 310mg, Fiber: 4g, Sugar: 13g, Vitamin C: 0mg, Calcium: 30mg, Iron: 1.7mg

Ingredients:
- 1/4 cup [40g] buckwheat flour
- 1/4 cup [60ml] unsweetened almond milk
- 1/4 cup [40g] chopped pitted Medjool dates
- 1/4 cup [60g] mashed ripe banana
- 1 tbsp ground flaxseed
- 1/4 tsp ground cinnamon
- 1/4 tsp baking powder
- 1/2 tsp olive oil

Directions:
1. Preheat the air fryer to 325°F [165°C].
2. In a mixing bowl, combine the mashed banana, almond milk, ground flaxseed, and olive oil. Stir until smooth.
3. Add the buckwheat flour, chopped dates, cinnamon, and baking powder to the wet mixture. Stir until just combined into a thick batter.
4. Spoon the batter evenly into two silicone mini muffin cups, filling them nearly to the top.
5. Place the muffin cups in the air fryer basket.
6. Cook for 15 minutes, or until a toothpick inserted into the center comes out clean and the tops are firm to the touch.
7. Let the muffins cool slightly before serving warm.

Avocado-Corn Breakfast Fritters

Time: 25 minutes
Serving Size: 2 servings
Prep Time: 10 minutes
Cook Time: 15 minutes

Each Serving Has:
Calories: 235, Carbohydrates: 26g, Saturated Fat: 1.1g, Protein: 5g, Fat: 13g, Sodium: 160mg, Potassium: 490mg, Fiber: 6g, Sugar: 3g, Vitamin C: 13mg, Calcium: 28mg, Iron: 1.5mg

Ingredients:
- 1/2 cup [80g] cooked and drained corn kernels
- 1/2 medium [70g] mashed ripe avocado
- 1/4 cup [30g] chopped red bell pepper
- 2 tbsp chopped red onion
- 2 tbsp rolled oats
- 1 tbsp ground flaxseed
- 1/4 tsp ground cumin
- 1/4 tsp garlic powder
- 1/4 tsp sea salt
- 1/8 tsp black pepper
- 1 tsp olive oil

Directions:
1. Preheat the air fryer to 375°F [190°C].
2. In a mixing bowl, combine the mashed avocado, cooked corn kernels, chopped bell pepper, onion, oats, ground flaxseed, cumin, garlic powder, sea salt, and black pepper. Mix thoroughly until the ingredients are evenly incorporated and the mixture forms a cohesive texture.
3. Shape the mixture into 2 round fritters, flattening slightly to about 1/2 inch [1.25 cm] thick.
4. Brush both sides of the fritters with olive oil.
5. Place the fritters in the air fryer basket, spacing them apart to ensure even cooking.
6. Cook for 15 minutes, flipping halfway through, until golden and crisp on the edges.
7. Let the fritters cool slightly before serving warm.

Mango Millet Breakfast Bites

⏰ **Time:** 30 minutes	🍽 **Serving Size:** 2 servings
🥗 **Prep Time:** 10 minutes	👨‍🍳 **Cook Time:** 20 minutes

Each Serving Has:
Calories: 225, Carbohydrates: 38g, Saturated Fat: 0.5g, Protein: 5g, Fat: 6g, Sodium: 80mg, Potassium: 340mg, Fiber: 4g, Sugar: 13g, Vitamin C: 18mg, Calcium: 28mg, Iron: 1.6mg

Ingredients:
- 1/2 cup [90g] cooked and cooled millet
- 1/4 cup [60g] mashed ripe mango
- 2 tbsp grated carrot
- 2 tbsp chopped raw walnuts
- 1 tbsp ground flaxseed
- 1/2 tsp ground cinnamon
- 1/4 tsp ground ginger
- 1/8 tsp sea salt
- 1/2 tsp olive oil

Directions:
1. Preheat the air fryer to 350°F [175°C].
2. In a mixing bowl, combine the cooked millet, mashed mango, grated carrot, chopped walnuts, ground flaxseed, cinnamon, ginger, and sea salt. Stir until a cohesive mixture forms.
3. Shape the mixture into 2 compact round bites, pressing firmly to hold their shape.
4. Lightly brush the outside of the bites with olive oil.
5. Place the bites in the air fryer basket, ensuring they are not touching.
6. Cook for 20 minutes, flipping gently halfway through, until golden brown and slightly crisp on the outside.
7. Let the bites cool slightly before serving warm.

Cauliflower-Potato Morning Tots

⏰ **Time:** 30 minutes	🍽 **Serving Size:** 2 servings
🥗 **Prep Time:** 10 minutes	👨‍🍳 **Cook Time:** 20 minutes

Each Serving Has:
Calories: 210, Carbohydrates: 33g, Saturated Fat: 0.5g, Protein: 5g, Fat: 6g, Sodium: 140mg, Potassium: 620mg, Fiber: 5g, Sugar: 2g, Vitamin C: 36mg, Calcium: 30mg, Iron: 2mg

Ingredients:
- 1/2 cup [90g] steamed and chopped cauliflower florets
- 1/2 cup [90g] mashed cooked yellow potato
- 1/4 cup [20g] rolled oats
- 1 tbsp chopped green onion
- 1 tbsp ground flaxseed
- 1/2 tsp garlic powder
- 1/4 tsp sea salt
- 1/8 tsp black pepper
- 1 tsp olive oil

Directions:
1. Preheat the air fryer to 375°F [190°C].
2. In a mixing bowl, combine the chopped cauliflower florets, mashed cooked potato, oats, chopped green onion, ground flaxseed, garlic powder, sea salt, and black pepper. Stir until a thick and uniform mixture forms.
3. Form the mixture into 6 small, oval-shaped tots by rolling and gently pressing them between your palms.
4. Brush the tots lightly with olive oil on all sides.
5. Arrange the tots in a single layer in the air fryer basket, leaving space between them for even cooking.
6. Cook for 20 minutes, flipping the tots halfway through, until golden and crisp on the outside.
7. Let the tots cool slightly before serving warm.

Air-Fried Berry Oat Clusters

Time: 25 minutes
Serving Size: 2 servings
Prep Time: 10 minutes
Cook Time: 15 minutes

Each Serving Has:
Calories: 215, Carbohydrates: 35g, Saturated Fat: 0.7g, Protein: 5g, Fat: 6g, Sodium: 65mg, Potassium: 290mg, Fiber: 5g, Sugar: 10g, Vitamin C: 6mg, Calcium: 30mg, Iron: 1.4mg

Ingredients:
- 1/2 cup [45g] rolled oats
- 1/4 cup [35g] mashed ripe banana
- 1/4 cup [40g] fresh or thawed mixed berries
- 2 tbsp chopped raw almonds
- 1 tbsp ground flaxseed
- 1/2 tsp ground cinnamon
- 1/2 tsp olive oil

Directions:
1. Preheat the air fryer to 350°F [175°C].
2. In a bowl, combine the mashed banana, mixed berries, oats, chopped almonds, ground flaxseed, and cinnamon. Mix well until the ingredients are evenly combined and form a sticky mixture.
3. Use your hands or a spoon to form two compact clusters, gently pressing them into a domed shape.
4. Lightly brush the outside of each cluster with olive oil.
5. Place the clusters in the air fryer basket, leaving space between them.
6. Cook for 15 minutes, or until the clusters are golden brown and firm to the touch.
7. Let the clusters cool for 5 minutes before serving warm.

Broccoli-Chickpea Mini Cakes

Time: 30 minutes
Serving Size: 2 servings
Prep Time: 10 minutes
Cook Time: 20 minutes

Each Serving Has:
Calories: 235, Carbohydrates: 28g, Saturated Fat: 0.7g, Protein: 9g, Fat: 9g, Sodium: 220mg, Potassium: 510mg, Fiber: 7g, Sugar: 3g, Vitamin C: 42mg, Calcium: 55mg, Iron: 2.3mg

Ingredients:
- 1/2 cup [85g] cooked chickpeas, rinsed and drained
- 1/2 cup [50g] steamed and chopped broccoli florets
- 2 tbsp chopped red onion
- 2 tbsp rolled oats
- 1 tbsp ground flaxseed
- 1 tbsp chopped fresh parsley
- 1/2 tsp garlic powder
- 1/4 tsp ground cumin
- 1/4 tsp sea salt
- 1/8 tsp black pepper
- 1 tsp olive oil

Directions:
1. Preheat the air fryer to 375°F [190°C].
2. In a bowl, mash the cooked chickpeas until they are they are mostly smooth, with some texture remaining.
3. Add the chopped broccoli florets, onion, oats, ground flaxseed, parsley, garlic powder, cumin, sea salt, and black pepper. Mix thoroughly until the mixture forms a cohesive texture.
4. Form the mixture into 2 compact mini cakes, flattening each to about 1 inch [2.5 cm] thick.
5. Brush both sides of the cakes lightly with olive oil.
6. Place the cakes in the air fryer basket with space between them.
7. Cook for 20 minutes, flipping gently halfway through, until golden brown and firm to the touch.
8. Let the cakes cool slightly before serving warm.

Crunchy Peanut Butter Oat Bites

Time: 20 minutes
Serving Size: 2 servings
Prep Time: 5 minutes
Cook Time: 15 minutes

Each Serving Has:
Calories: 240, Carbohydrates: 28g, Saturated Fat: 1g, Protein: 7g, Fat: 11g, Sodium: 105mg, Potassium: 310mg, Fiber: 4g, Sugar: 5g, Vitamin C: 0mg, Calcium: 22mg, Iron: 1.4mg

Ingredients:
- 1/2 cup [45g] rolled oats
- 2 tbsp crunchy natural peanut butter
- 1/4 cup [60g] mashed ripe banana
- 1 tbsp ground flaxseed
- 1 tbsp chopped raw peanuts
- 1/2 tsp ground cinnamon

Directions:
1. Preheat the air fryer to 350°F [175°C].
2. In a mixing bowl, combine the mashed banana, peanut butter, oats, ground flaxseed, chopped peanuts, and cinnamon. Mix until a thick, sticky dough forms.
3. Shape the mixture into 2 round, slightly flattened bites.
4. Place the bites in the air fryer basket, leaving space between them.
5. Cook for 15 minutes, or until the edges are golden and the bites are firm to the touch.
6. Let the bites cool slightly before serving warm.

Golden Lentil Breakfast Bars

Time: 30 minutes
Serving Size: 2 servings
Prep Time: 10 minutes
Cook Time: 20 minutes

Each Serving Has:
Calories: 245, Carbohydrates: 34g, Saturated Fat: 0.6g, Protein: 11g, Fat: 7g, Sodium: 150mg, Potassium: 540mg, Fiber: 7g, Sugar: 3g, Vitamin C: 3mg, Calcium: 36mg, Iron: 2.5mg

Ingredients:
- 1/2 cup [100g] cooked red lentils, drained
- 1/4 cup [60g] mashed ripe banana
- 1/4 cup [25g] rolled oats
- 2 tbsp grated carrot
- 1 tbsp ground flaxseed
- 1 tbsp chopped raw pumpkin seeds
- 1/2 tsp ground turmeric
- 1/4 tsp sea salt
- 1/8 tsp black pepper

Directions:
1. Preheat the air fryer to 350°F [175°C].
2. In a mixing bowl, combine the cooked lentils, mashed banana, oats, grated carrot, ground flaxseed, chopped pumpkin seeds, turmeric, sea salt, and black pepper. Mix well until the mixture is fully incorporated and has thickened.
3. Shape the mixture into 2 rectangular bars and press firmly to hold their shape.
4. Place the bars in the air fryer basket with space between them.
5. Cook for 20 minutes, flipping halfway through, until they are golden and lightly crisp on the outside.
6. Let the bars cool for a few minutes before serving warm.

Savory Oat and Mushroom Balls

🕐	**Time:** 30 minutes	🍽	**Serving Size:** 2 servings
🥗	**Prep Time:** 10 minutes	👨‍🍳	**Cook Time:** 20 minutes

Each Serving Has:
Calories: 220, Carbohydrates: 28g, Saturated Fat: 0.6g, Protein: 7g, Fat: 9g, Sodium: 210mg, Potassium: 430mg, Fiber: 5g, Sugar: 2g, Vitamin C: 3mg, Calcium: 28mg, Iron: 2.2mg

Ingredients:
- 1/2 cup [50g] rolled oats
- 1/2 cup [75g] chopped cremini mushrooms
- 1/4 cup [40g] mashed cooked chickpeas
- 1 tbsp chopped yellow onion
- 1 tbsp ground flaxseed
- 1 tbsp chopped fresh parsley
- 1/2 tsp garlic powder
- 1/2 tsp dried thyme
- 1/8 tsp black pepper
- 1 tsp olive oil

Directions:
1. Preheat the air fryer to 375°F [190°C].
2. In a dry skillet over medium heat, sauté the chopped cremini mushrooms and onion for 3–4 minutes, until softened. Then, let them cool slightly.
3. In a mixing bowl, combine the oats, mashed chickpeas, sautéed mushrooms and onion, ground flaxseed, chopped parsley, garlic powder, thyme, and black pepper. Mix until the mixture holds together when pressed.
4. Form the mixture into 6 compact balls, pressing firmly to shape.
5. Brush the surface of each ball lightly with olive oil.
6. Place the balls in the air fryer basket, spaced apart.
7. Cook for 20 minutes, shaking the basket gently halfway through, until the outsides are crisp and golden.
8. Let the balls cool slightly before serving warm.

Air-Fried Polenta Slices

🕐	**Time:** 25 minutes	🍽	**Serving Size:** 2 servings
🥗	**Prep Time:** 10 minutes	👨‍🍳	**Cook Time:** 15 minutes

Each Serving Has:
Calories: 190, Carbohydrates: 27g, Saturated Fat: 0.4g, Protein: 4g, Fat: 7g, Sodium: 160mg, Potassium: 120mg, Fiber: 2g, Sugar: 1g, Vitamin C: 0mg, Calcium: 6mg, Iron: 1.2mg

Ingredients:
- 1 cup [240g] cooked and cooled firm polenta
- 1 tbsp chopped fresh parsley
- 1/2 tsp garlic powder
- 1/4 tsp smoked paprika
- 1/4 tsp sea salt
- 1/8 tsp black pepper
- 1 tsp olive oil

Directions:
1. Preheat the air fryer to 375°F [190°C].
2. Slice the cooked polenta into 4 equal rectangles, each about 1/2 inch [1.25 cm] thick.
3. In a bowl, gently toss the polenta slices with the chopped parsley, garlic powder, smoked paprika, sea salt, and black pepper until evenly coated.
4. Lightly brush the air fryer basket with the olive oil.
5. Arrange the slices in a single layer in the air fryer basket, ensuring they do not touch.
6. Cook for 15 minutes, flipping the slices halfway through, until the outsides are golden and crisp.
7. Let the slices cool slightly before serving warm.

CHAPTER 2: BREAKFASTS ◊ 23

Sweet Beet & Walnut Crisps

- **Time:** 25 minutes
- **Serving Size:** 2 servings
- **Prep Time:** 10 minutes
- **Cook Time:** 15 minutes

Each Serving Has:
Calories: 210, Carbohydrates: 20g, Saturated Fat: 0.6g, Protein: 5g, Fat: 13g, Sodium: 120mg, Potassium: 470mg, Fiber: 5g, Sugar: 9g, Vitamin C: 6mg, Calcium: 35mg, Iron: 1.5mg

Ingredients:
- 1 cup [100g] peeled and grated raw beet
- 1/4 cup [30g] chopped raw walnuts
- 1/4 cup [25g] rolled oats
- 2 tbsp ground flaxseed
- 1 tbsp mashed ripe banana
- 1/2 tsp ground cinnamon
- 1/4 tsp sea salt
- 1/2 tsp olive oil

Directions:
1. Preheat the air fryer to 350°F [175°C].
2. In a mixing bowl, combine the grated beet, chopped walnuts, oats, ground flaxseed, mashed banana, cinnamon, and sea salt. Mix until fully incorporated and slightly sticky.
3. Divide the mixture into small portions and flatten each into thin, round crisps, about 2 inches [5 cm] in diameter and 1/4 inch [0.6 cm] thick.
4. Lightly brush the air fryer basket with the olive oil.
5. Arrange the crisps in a single layer in the air fryer basket, leaving space between each one.
6. Cook for 15 minutes, flipping halfway through, until edges are crisp and lightly browned.
7. Let the crisps cool slightly before serving warm.

Parsnip & Leek Hash Cups

- **Time:** 30 minutes
- **Serving Size:** 2 servings
- **Prep Time:** 10 minutes
- **Cook Time:** 20 minutes

Each Serving Has:
Calories: 215, Carbohydrates: 30g, Saturated Fat: 0.6g, Protein: 4g, Fat: 9g, Sodium: 190mg, Potassium: 580mg, Fiber: 6g, Sugar: 8g, Vitamin C: 20mg, Calcium: 45mg, Iron: 1.8mg

Ingredients:
- 1 cup [100g] peeled and grated parsnip
- 1/2 cup [50g] chopped leek, white and light green parts only
- 1/4 cup [25g] rolled oats
- 1 tbsp ground flaxseed
- 1 tbsp chopped fresh parsley
- 1/2 tsp garlic powder
- 1/4 tsp sea salt
- 1/8 tsp black pepper
- 1 tsp olive oil

Directions:
1. Preheat the air fryer to 375°F [190°C].
2. In a mixing bowl, combine the grated parsnip, chopped leek, parsley, oats, ground flaxseed, garlic powder, sea salt, and black pepper. Mix thoroughly until the mixture forms a cohesive texture.
3. Divide the mixture in half and press each portion into silicone muffin cups, shaping them into small cup-like forms with a slight well in the center.
4. Brush the tops and edges of the hash cups lightly with olive oil.
5. Place the filled muffin cups in the air fryer basket.
6. Cook for 20 minutes, or until golden brown and firm to the touch.
7. Let it cool slightly before carefully removing from the cups.

Quinoa-Pumpkin Mini Loaves

Time: 30 minutes
Serving Size: 2 servings
Prep Time: 10 minutes
Cook Time: 20 minutes

Each Serving Has:
Calories: 230, Carbohydrates: 33g, Saturated Fat: 0.5g, Protein: 7g, Fat: 8g, Sodium: 160mg, Potassium: 460mg, Fiber: 5g, Sugar: 4g, Vitamin C: 3mg, Calcium: 34mg, Iron: 2.2mg

Ingredients:
- 1/2 cup [90g] cooked quinoa
- 1/3 cup [80g] unsweetened pumpkin purée
- 1/4 cup [25g] rolled oats
- 2 tbsp chopped raw walnuts
- 1 tbsp ground flaxseed
- 1/2 tsp ground cinnamon
- 1/4 tsp ground ginger
- 1/4 tsp sea salt
- 1/8 tsp ground nutmeg
- 1/2 tsp olive oil

Directions:
1. Preheat the air fryer to 350°F [175°C].
2. In a mixing bowl, combine the cooked quinoa, pumpkin purée, oats, chopped walnuts, ground flaxseed, cinnamon, ginger, sea salt, and nutmeg. Stir until the mixture is thick and evenly combined.
3. Lightly grease two small silicone mini loaf molds with olive oil.
4. Divide the mixture evenly between the molds, pressing down to compact and shape into firm loaves.
5. Place the molds in the air fryer basket.
6. Cook for 20 minutes, or until the tops are golden and firm to the touch.
7. Let the loaves cool for 5 minutes before carefully removing them from the molds.

Green Pea and Herb Medallions

Time: 25 minutes
Serving Size: 2 servings
Prep Time: 10 minutes
Cook Time: 15 minutes

Each Serving Has:
Calories: 210, Carbohydrates: 28g, Saturated Fat: 0.5g, Protein: 8g, Fat: 8g, Sodium: 180mg, Potassium: 460mg, Fiber: 6g, Sugar: 5g, Vitamin C: 17mg, Calcium: 38mg, Iron: 2.1mg

Ingredients:
- 3/4 cup [110g] thawed frozen green peas
- 1/4 cup [40g] mashed cooked chickpeas
- 1/4 cup [25g] rolled oats
- 2 tbsp chopped fresh parsley
- 1 tbsp chopped fresh dill
- 1 tbsp ground flaxseed
- 1/2 tsp garlic powder
- 1/4 tsp sea salt
- 1/8 tsp black pepper
- 1 tsp olive oil

Directions:
1. Preheat the air fryer to 375°F [190°C].
2. In a food processor or a bowl, mash the green peas until partially broken down.
3. Add the mashed chickpeas, oats, chopped parsley, dill, ground flaxseed, garlic powder, sea salt, and black pepper. Pulse or stir until a thick, chunky mixture forms that holds together when pressed.
4. Divide the mixture into 4 equal portions and shape each into a round, flat medallion about 1/2 inch [1.25 cm] thick.
5. Brush both sides of each medallion lightly with olive oil.
6. Place the medallions in the air fryer basket in a single layer, with space between each.
7. Cook for 15 minutes, flipping halfway through, until crisp and lightly golden.
8. Let the medallions cool slightly before serving.

CHAPTER 2: BREAKFASTS ◊ 25

Coconut-Chia Breakfast Rolls

⏲ **Time:** 30 minutes	🍽 **Serving Size:** 2 servings
🥗 **Prep Time:** 10 minutes	👨‍🍳 **Cook Time:** 20 minutes

Each Serving Has:
Calories: 240, Carbohydrates: 30g, Saturated Fat: 3.2g, Protein: 6g, Fat: 11g, Sodium: 135mg, Potassium: 290mg, Fiber: 6g, Sugar: 5g, Vitamin C: 1mg, Calcium: 80mg, Iron: 2mg

Ingredients:
- 1/2 cup [60g] rolled oats
- 1/4 cup [60ml] unsweetened coconut milk
- 1/4 cup [60g] mashed ripe banana
- 2 tbsp unsweetened shredded coconut
- 1 tbsp chia seeds
- 1 tbsp ground flaxseed
- 1/2 tsp ground cinnamon
- 1/8 tsp sea salt
- 1 tsp olive oil

Directions:
1. Preheat the air fryer to 350°F [175°C].
2. In a mixing bowl, combine the oats, coconut milk, mashed banana, shredded coconut, chia seeds, ground flaxseed, cinnamon, and sea salt. Stir until a thick, sticky dough forms. Let rest for 5 minutes to allow the chia and flax to absorb moisture.
3. Divide the mixture into two equal portions. With slightly damp hands, shape each into a small roll about 2 inches [5 cm] in diameter.
4. Brush the outside of each roll lightly with olive oil.
5. Place the rolls in the air fryer basket with space between them.
6. Cook for 20 minutes, flipping the rolls halfway through, until they are golden and lightly crisp on the outside.
7. Let the rolls cool slightly before serving warm.

Spiced Butternut Breakfast Fries

⏲ **Time:** 30 minutes	🍽 **Serving Size:** 2 servings
🥗 **Prep Time:** 10 minutes	👨‍🍳 **Cook Time:** 20 minutes

Each Serving Has:
Calories: 190, Carbohydrates: 30g, Saturated Fat: 0.6g, Protein: 3g, Fat: 7g, Sodium: 170mg, Potassium: 540mg, Fiber: 5g, Sugar: 7g, Vitamin C: 26mg, Calcium: 52mg, Iron: 1.2mg

Ingredients:
- 2 cups [260g] peeled and cut butternut squash sticks (1/4-inch thick)
- 1 tbsp olive oil
- 1/2 tsp ground cinnamon
- 1/4 tsp ground cumin
- 1/4 tsp smoked paprika
- 1/4 tsp sea salt
- 1/8 tsp black pepper

Directions:
1. Preheat the air fryer to 375°F [190°C].
2. In a mixing bowl, toss the butternut squash sticks with olive oil, cinnamon, cumin, smoked paprika, sea salt, and black pepper until evenly coated.
3. Arrange the spiced squash sticks in a single layer in the air fryer basket, ensuring they do not overlap.
4. Cook for 20 minutes, shaking the basket halfway through to ensure even crisping.
5. Remove the fries from the air fryer and serve.

Air-Fried Apple Buckwheat Slices

⏰ Time: 25 minutes	🍽 Serving Size: 2 servings
🥗 Prep Time: 10 minutes	👨‍🍳 Cook Time: 15 minutes

Each Serving Has:
Calories: 215, Carbohydrates: 36g, Saturated Fat: 0.6g, Protein: 5g, Fat: 7g, Sodium: 105mg, Potassium: 310mg, Fiber: 5g, Sugar: 9g, Vitamin C: 5mg, Calcium: 28mg, Iron: 1.7mg

Ingredients:
- 1/2 cup [90g] mashed cooked buckwheat
- 1/2 cup [75g] grated sweet apple, peeled
- 2 tbsp buckwheat flour
- 1 tbsp ground flaxseed
- 1/2 tsp ground cinnamon
- 1/4 tsp sea salt
- 1/2 tsp olive oil

Directions:
1. Preheat the air fryer to 350°F [175°C].
2. In a mixing bowl, combine the mashed buckwheat, grated apple, buckwheat flour, ground flaxseed, cinnamon, and sea salt. Stir well until the mixture forms a soft, moldable dough.
3. Divide the dough into 4 equal portions and shape each into a flat oval slice about 1/2 inch [1.25 cm] thick.
4. Lightly brush both sides of each slice with olive oil.
5. Arrange the slices in a single layer in the air fryer basket, leaving space between them.
6. Cook for 15 minutes, flipping halfway through, until the edges are crisp and the slices are lightly golden.
7. Let the slices cool slightly before serving warm.

Tomato-Basil Breakfast Triangles

⏰ Time: 25 minutes	🍽 Serving Size: 2 servings
🥗 Prep Time: 10 minutes	👨‍🍳 Cook Time: 15 minutes

Each Serving Has:
Calories: 210, Carbohydrates: 28g, Saturated Fat: 0.8g, Protein: 6g, Fat: 8g, Sodium: 190mg, Potassium: 410mg, Fiber: 5g, Sugar: 4g, Vitamin C: 9mg, Calcium: 35mg, Iron: 2.1mg

Ingredients:
- 1/2 cup [100g] cooked and cooled quinoa
- 1/2 cup [75g] chopped ripe tomato
- 1/4 cup [25g] rolled oats
- 2 tbsp chopped fresh basil
- 1 tbsp ground flaxseed
- 1/2 tsp garlic powder
- 1/8 tsp sea salt
- 1 tsp olive oil

Directions:
1. Preheat the air fryer to 375°F [190°C].
2. In a mixing bowl, combine the cooked quinoa, chopped tomato, oats, basil, ground flaxseed, garlic powder, and sea salt. Stir until the mixture holds together well.
3. Divide the mixture into 2 portions. Flatten each into a thick triangle, then cut each triangle in half to form 4 smaller triangles.
4. Lightly brush each triangle on both sides with olive oil.
5. Arrange the triangles in the air fryer basket in a single layer, ensuring they do not overlap.
6. Cook for 15 minutes, flipping halfway through, until golden and firm.
7. Let the triangles cool slightly before serving warm.

Millet-Cinnamon Crunch Wedges

Time: 30 minutes
Serving Size: 2 servings
Prep Time: 10 minutes
Cook Time: 20 minutes

Each Serving Has:
Calories: 225, Carbohydrates: 34g, Saturated Fat: 1g, Protein: 6g, Fat: 7g, Sodium: 130mg, Potassium: 240mg, Fiber: 4g, Sugar: 5g, Vitamin C: 1mg, Calcium: 28mg, Iron: 1.9mg

Ingredients:
- 1/2 cup [95g] cooked and cooled millet
- 1/3 cup [80g] mashed ripe banana
- 2 tbsp rolled oats
- 1 tbsp ground flaxseed
- 1 tbsp unsweetened shredded coconut
- 1 tsp ground cinnamon
- 1/4 tsp sea salt
- 1/2 tsp olive oil

Directions:
1. Preheat the air fryer to 350°F [175°C].
2. In a mixing bowl, combine the cooked millet, mashed banana, oats, ground flaxseed, shredded coconut, cinnamon, and sea salt. Stir until the mixture holds together and forms a sticky, dough-like consistency.
3. Press the dough into a flat 1/2-inch [1.25 cm] thick circle on a piece of parchment paper. Cut into 4 wedge-shaped triangles.
4. Lightly brush the tops of the wedges with olive oil.
5. Place the wedges in the air fryer basket in a single layer, using parchment if needed to prevent sticking.
6. Cook for 20 minutes, flipping halfway through, until crisp and golden on the edges.
7. Let the wedges cool slightly before serving warm.

Chapter 3: Snacks

Crispy Chickpea Snack Bombs

Time: 25 minutes	Serving Size: 2 servings
Prep Time: 10 minutes	Cook Time: 15 minutes

Each Serving Has:
Calories: 220, Carbohydrates: 28g, Saturated Fat: 0.6g, Protein: 9g, Fat: 7g, Sodium: 180mg, Potassium: 390mg, Fiber: 6g, Sugar: 3g, Vitamin C: 2mg, Calcium: 41mg, Iron: 2.3mg

Ingredients:
- 3/4 cup [130g] mashed cooked chickpeas
- 1/4 cup [25g] rolled oats
- 2 tbsp grated carrot
- 1 tbsp chopped fresh parsley
- 1 tbsp ground flaxseed
- 1/2 tsp garlic powder
- 1/4 tsp smoked paprika
- 1/8 tsp sea salt
- 1/8 tsp black pepper
- 1 tsp olive oil

Directions:
1. Preheat the air fryer to 375°F [190°C].
2. In a mixing bowl, combine the mashed chickpeas, oats, grated carrot, chopped parsley, ground flaxseed, garlic powder, smoked paprika, sea salt, and black pepper. Stir well until the mixture forms a cohesive texture.
3. Divide the mixture into 8 equal portions and roll each into a compact ball.
4. Lightly brush the surface of each ball with olive oil.
5. Place the chickpea balls in the air fryer basket in a single layer, leaving space between them.
6. Cook for 15 minutes, shaking the basket halfway through, until the snack bombs are golden and crispy.
7. Let the bombs cool slightly before serving warm.

Air-Fried Carrot Zucchini Chips

Time: 25 minutes	Serving Size: 2 servings
Prep Time: 10 minutes	Cook Time: 15 minutes

Each Serving Has:
Calories: 130, Carbohydrates: 14g, Saturated Fat: 0.5g, Protein: 3g, Fat: 7g, Sodium: 150mg, Potassium: 450mg, Fiber: 4g, Sugar: 5g, Vitamin C: 9mg, Calcium: 33mg, Iron: 1.2mg

Ingredients:
- 1 cup [110g] thinly sliced zucchini
- 1 cup [100g] thinly sliced carrot
- 1 tbsp ground flaxseed
- 1 tbsp olive oil
- 1/2 tsp garlic powder
- 1/4 tsp smoked paprika
- 1/8 tsp sea salt

Directions:
1. Preheat the air fryer to 375°F [190°C].
2. In a large bowl, toss the thinly sliced zucchini and carrot with ground flaxseed, olive oil, garlic powder, smoked paprika, and sea salt until well coated.
3. Arrange the slices in a single layer in the air fryer basket, working in batches if necessary to avoid overlap.
4. Cook for 15 minutes, shaking the basket halfway through, until the chips are golden and crisp at the edges.
5. Let the chips cool for 5 minutes before serving.

Apple-Cinnamon Wedge Bites

Time: 22 minutes	Serving Size: 2 servings
Prep Time: 7 minutes	Cook Time: 15 minutes

Each Serving Has:
Calories: 142, Carbohydrates: 28g, Saturated Fat: 0.5g, Protein: 2g, Fat: 3g, Sodium: 65mg, Potassium: 190mg, Fiber: 4g, Sugar: 17g, Vitamin C: 7mg, Calcium: 22mg, Iron: 0.5mg

Ingredients:
- 2 medium crisp apples, cut into wedges
- 1 tbsp ground flaxseed
- 1 tsp olive oil
- 1/2 tsp ground cinnamon
- 1/4 tsp ground ginger

Directions:
1. Preheat the air fryer to 375°F [190°C].
2. In a bowl, toss the apple wedges with ground flaxseed, olive oil, cinnamon, and ginger until evenly coated.
3. Arrange the apple wedges in a single layer in the air fryer basket, leaving space between each wedge for airflow.
4. Air fry for 15 minutes, flipping halfway through, until the apples are golden and lightly crisp on the edges.
5. Let the wedges cool slightly before serving.

Curried Lentil Poppers

Time: 28 minutes
Serving Size: 2 servings
Prep Time: 10 minutes
Cook Time: 18 minutes

Each Serving Has:
Calories: 176, Carbohydrates: 25g, Saturated Fat: 0.4g, Protein: 10g, Fat: 4g, Sodium: 178mg, Potassium: 472mg, Fiber: 9g, Sugar: 2g, Vitamin C: 5mg, Calcium: 39mg, Iron: 3mg

Ingredients:
- 1 cup [180g] cooked green lentils, drained
- 1/4 cup [30g] grated carrot
- 1/4 cup [40g] chopped red onion
- 1 tbsp ground flaxseed
- 1 tbsp chickpea flour
- 1 tsp curry powder
- 1/4 tsp ground cumin
- 1/4 tsp garlic powder
- 1/8 tsp sea salt

Directions:
1. Preheat the air fryer to 375°F [190°C].
2. In a mixing bowl, combine the cooked lentils, grated carrot, chopped onion, ground flaxseed, chickpea flour, curry powder, cumin, garlic powder, and sea salt. Mash the mixture with a fork or potato masher until it holds together but still has some texture.
3. Form the mixture into small round poppers, about the size of a tablespoon each, and gently press to compact them.
4. Arrange the lentil poppers in a single layer in the air fryer basket, leaving space between each one.
5. Air fry for 18 minutes, flipping halfway through, until golden and crisp on the outside.
6. Let the poppers cool slightly before serving.

Sweet Potato Toast Fingers

Time: 25 minutes
Serving Size: 2 servings
Prep Time: 5 minutes
Cook Time: 20 minutes

Each Serving Has:
Calories: 164, Carbohydrates: 36g, Saturated Fat: 0.3g, Protein: 2g, Fat: 2g, Sodium: 74mg, Potassium: 470mg, Fiber: 5g, Sugar: 7g, Vitamin C: 5mg, Calcium: 31mg, Iron: 0.8mg

Ingredients:
- 1 large [250g] peeled sweet potato
- 1 tsp olive oil
- 1/4 tsp ground ginger
- 1/8 tsp ground cardamom
- 1/8 tsp ground nutmeg
- 1/8 tsp sea salt
- 2 tbsp almond butter
- 1 tbsp maple syrup
- 1/4 tsp ground cinnamon
- 1–2 tbsp unsweetened almond milk

Directions:
1. Preheat the air fryer to 375°F [190°C].
2. Slice the sweet potato lengthwise into 1/4-inch [0.6cm] thick planks, then cut each plank into even toast-sized fingers.
3. In a bowl, toss the sweet potato fingers with olive oil, ginger, cardamom, nutmeg, and sea salt until well coated.
4. Arrange the sweet potato fingers in a single layer in the air fryer basket.
5. Air fry for 20 minutes, flipping the food once halfway through, until the edges are golden and the centers are tender.
6. Meanwhile, in a small bowl, stir together the almond butter, maple syrup, cinnamon, and 1–2 tablespoons of almond milk until smooth and creamy.
7. Let the sweet potato fingers cool slightly, then serve alongside the maple-cinnamon dip.

Seasoned Green Pea Crunch

⏱ Time: 20 minutes	🍽 Serving Size: 2 servings
🥗 Prep Time: 5 minutes	👨‍🍳 Cook Time: 15 minutes

Each Serving Has:
Calories: 132, Carbohydrates: 18g, Saturated Fat: 0.3g, Protein: 7g, Fat: 4g, Sodium: 210mg, Potassium: 290mg, Fiber: 6g, Sugar: 3g, Vitamin C: 12mg, Calcium: 25mg, Iron: 1.9mg

Ingredients:
- 1 1/2 cups [230g] thawed frozen green peas, patted dry
- 1 tsp olive oil
- 1/2 tsp garlic powder
- 1/4 tsp smoked paprika
- 1/4 tsp sea salt

Directions:
1. Preheat the air fryer to 375°F [190°C].
2. In a bowl, toss the green peas with olive oil, garlic powder, smoked paprika, and sea salt until evenly coated.
3. Arrange the peas in a single layer in the air fryer basket.
4. Air fry for 15 minutes, shaking the basket every 5 minutes for even crisping.
5. Let the pea crunch cool for a few minutes before serving.

Roasted Cauliflower Nuggets

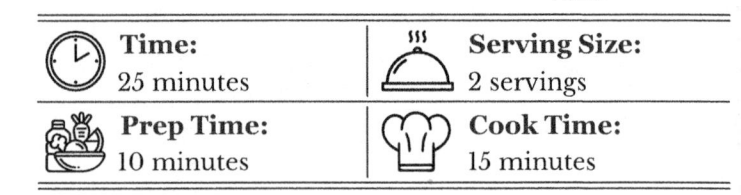

⏱ Time: 25 minutes	🍽 Serving Size: 2 servings
🥗 Prep Time: 10 minutes	👨‍🍳 Cook Time: 15 minutes

Each Serving Has:
Calories: 138, Carbohydrates: 14g, Saturated Fat: 0.6g, Protein: 5g, Fat: 7g, Sodium: 210mg, Potassium: 460mg, Fiber: 5g, Sugar: 4g, Vitamin C: 73mg, Calcium: 40mg, Iron: 1.2mg

Ingredients:
- 2 cups [200g] bite-sized cauliflower florets
- 1 tbsp olive oil
- 2 tbsp almond flour
- 1/2 tsp smoked paprika
- 1/4 tsp garlic powder
- 1/4 tsp onion powder
- 1/8 tsp sea salt

Directions:
1. Preheat the air fryer to 375°F [190°C].
2. In a mixing bowl, toss the cauliflower florets with olive oil until lightly coated.
3. In a small bowl, mix the almond flour, smoked paprika, garlic powder, onion powder, and sea salt.
4. Sprinkle the seasoning mix evenly over the oiled cauliflower and toss to coat.
5. Arrange the coated cauliflower in a single layer in the air fryer basket.
6. Air fry for 15 minutes, shaking the basket halfway through to ensure even roasting.
7. Let the nuggets cool slightly before serving warm.

Corn & Black Bean Snack Balls

Time: 25 minutes
Serving Size: 2 servings
Prep Time: 10 minutes
Cook Time: 15 minutes

Each Serving Has:
Calories: 182, Carbohydrates: 24g, Saturated Fat: 0.6g, Protein: 7g, Fat: 6g, Sodium: 216mg, Potassium: 394mg, Fiber: 7g, Sugar: 2g, Vitamin C: 10mg, Calcium: 34mg, Iron: 2mg

Ingredients:
- 1/2 cup [85g] cooked black beans, rinsed and drained
- 1/2 cup [80g] cooked sweet corn kernels
- 1/4 cup [25g] chopped red bell pepper
- 2 tbsp chopped red onion
- 1/4 cup [20g] rolled oats
- 1 tbsp chopped fresh cilantro
- 1/2 tsp ground cumin
- 1/4 tsp garlic powder
- 1/8 tsp sea salt
- 1 tsp olive oil

Directions:
1. Preheat the air fryer to 375°F [190°C].
2. In a medium bowl, mash the black beans with a fork until mostly smooth but still slightly chunky.
3. Add the cooked corn kernels, chopped bell pepper, onion, oats, cilantro, cumin, garlic powder, and sea salt. Mix thoroughly until a cohesive mixture forms.
4. Using clean hands, form the mixture into 12 small, compact snack balls.
5. Lightly brush the air fryer basket. Place the balls in a single layer, leaving space between each one.
6. Air fry for 15 minutes, shaking the basket gently halfway through, until the edges are crispy and golden.
7. Let the snack balls cool slightly before serving warm.

Crunchy Quinoa Clusters

Time: 30 minutes
Serving Size: 2 servings
Prep Time: 10 minutes
Cook Time: 20 minutes

Each Serving Has:
Calories: 186, Carbohydrates: 25g, Saturated Fat: 0.7g, Protein: 6g, Fat: 6g, Sodium: 104mg, Potassium: 292mg, Fiber: 4g, Sugar: 3g, Vitamin C: 1mg, Calcium: 32mg, Iron: 2mg

Ingredients:
- 1/2 cup [90g] cooked and cooled quinoa
- 1/4 cup [20g] rolled oats
- 1/4 cup [30g] grated carrot
- 2 tbsp mashed ripe banana
- 1 tbsp raw sunflower seeds
- 1/2 tsp ground cinnamon
- 1/4 tsp ground ginger
- 1/8 tsp sea salt

Directions:
1. Preheat the air fryer to 350°F [175°C].
2. In a medium bowl, combine the cooked quinoa, oats, grated carrot, mashed banana, sunflower seeds, cinnamon, ginger, and sea salt. Mix until well combined and slightly sticky.
3. Scoop out portions and gently form them into compact clusters, each about one tablespoon in size.
4. Arrange the clusters in a single layer in the air fryer basket, leaving space between each for air circulation.
5. Air fry for 20 minutes, flipping them gently halfway through, until golden brown and crisp around the edges.
6. Let the clusters cool for 5 minutes before serving.

Parsnip & Herb Wedges

⏲ Time: 30 minutes	🍽 Serving Size: 2 servings
🥗 Prep Time: 10 minutes	👨‍🍳 Cook Time: 20 minutes

Each Serving Has:
Calories: 162, Carbohydrates: 28g, Saturated Fat: 0.6g, Protein: 2g, Fat: 5g, Sodium: 190mg, Potassium: 510mg, Fiber: 6g, Sugar: 7g, Vitamin C: 17mg, Calcium: 50mg, Iron: 1mg

Ingredients:
- 2 cups [260g] peeled and wedged parsnips
- 1 tbsp olive oil
- 1 tsp chopped fresh rosemary
- 1/2 tsp dried thyme
- 1/4 tsp garlic powder
- 1/4 tsp sea salt

Directions:
1. Preheat the air fryer to 375°F [190°C].
2. In a mixing bowl, toss the parsnip wedges with olive oil, chopped rosemary, thyme, garlic powder, and sea salt until evenly coated.
3. Arrange the wedges in a single layer in the air fryer basket, ensuring they do not overlap.
4. Cook for 20 minutes, shaking the basket halfway through, until the wedges are golden and crisp at the edges.
5. Remove the wedges from the air fryer and serve.

Plantain & Walnut Munchies

⏲ Time: 25 minutes	🍽 Serving Size: 2 servings
🥗 Prep Time: 10 minutes	👨‍🍳 Cook Time: 15 minutes

Each Serving Has:
Calories: 210, Carbohydrates: 29g, Saturated Fat: 1.3g, Protein: 3g, Fat: 10g, Sodium: 60mg, Potassium: 540mg, Fiber: 3g, Sugar: 13g, Vitamin C: 14mg, Calcium: 25mg, Iron: 1mg

Ingredients:
- 1 medium [150g] ripe plantain, peeled and sliced into 1/4-inch rounds
- 1/4 cup [30g] chopped raw walnuts
- 1/2 tsp ground cinnamon
- 1/4 tsp ground ginger
- 1/2 tbsp olive oil

Directions:
1. Preheat the air fryer to 375°F [190°C].
2. In a bowl, toss the plantain slices with olive oil, cinnamon, and ginger until evenly coated.
3. Gently fold in the chopped walnuts, making sure they adhere lightly to the plantain slices.
4. Arrange the coated plantain slices in a single layer in the air fryer basket.
5. Cook for 15 minutes, flipping the slices once halfway through, until they are golden and crisp at the edges.
6. Remove the munchies from the air fryer and serve.

Tofu-Celery Air Sticks

Time: 30 minutes
Serving Size: 2 servings
Prep Time: 15 minutes
Cook Time: 15 minutes

Each Serving Has:
Calories: 188, Carbohydrates: 7g, Saturated Fat: 1g, Protein: 14g, Fat: 12g, Sodium: 210mg, Potassium: 380mg, Fiber: 2g, Sugar: 2g, Vitamin C: 4mg, Calcium: 230mg, Iron: 2.4mg

Ingredients:
- 1 cup [150g] firm tofu, pressed and sliced into 3-inch sticks
- 1/2 cup [50g] grated celery
- 1/4 cup [25g] ground rolled oats
- 1 tbsp nutritional yeast
- 1/2 tsp garlic powder
- 1/2 tsp smoked paprika
- 1/2 tbsp olive oil

Directions:
1. Preheat the air fryer to 375°F [190°C].
2. In a bowl, combine the grated celery, nutritional yeast, garlic powder, and smoked paprika.
3. Add the tofu sticks and toss gently to coat with the celery mixture.
4. Sprinkle the ground oats over the tofu mixture and toss again until the tofu is evenly coated.
5. Drizzle with the olive oil and gently toss to bind the coating.
6. Arrange the tofu sticks in a single layer in the air fryer basket.
7. Cook for 15 minutes, flipping once halfway through, until golden and crisp.
8. Remove the sticks from the air fryer and serve.

Sweet Date-Coconut Balls

Time: 22 minutes
Serving Size: 2 servings
Prep Time: 10 minutes
Cook Time: 12 minutes

Each Serving Has:
Calories: 212, Carbohydrates: 32g, Saturated Fat: 5g, Protein: 3g, Fat: 9g, Sodium: 2mg, Potassium: 315mg, Fiber: 5g, Sugar: 23g, Vitamin C: 0mg, Calcium: 34mg, Iron: 1mg

Ingredients:
- 1/2 cup [90g] pitted soft Medjool dates, chopped
- 1/3 cup [30g] shredded unsweetened coconut
- 1/4 cup [25g] rolled oats
- 1 tbsp ground flaxseed
- 1/4 tsp ground cinnamon
- 1/2 tsp vanilla extract
- 1/2 tsp olive oil

Directions:
1. Preheat the air fryer to 325°F [165°C].
2. In a food processor, combine the chopped dates, shredded coconut, oats, ground flaxseed, cinnamon, and vanilla extract.
3. Pulse until the mixture forms a slightly sticky, coarse dough.
4. Lightly grease your palms with the olive oil and roll the mixture into 12 small balls.
5. Arrange the balls in a single layer in the air fryer basket, leaving space between them.
6. Air fry for 12 minutes, shaking the basket halfway through for even browning.
7. Let the balls cool for 5 minutes before serving.

Spicy Mushroom Snack Cubes

⏲ Time: 30 minutes	🍽 Serving Size: 2 servings
🥗 Prep Time: 15 minutes	👨‍🍳 Cook Time: 15 minutes

Each Serving Has:
Calories: 138, Carbohydrates: 11g, Saturated Fat: 1g, Protein: 7g, Fat: 7g, Sodium: 191mg, Potassium: 420mg, Fiber: 3g, Sugar: 3g, Vitamin C: 6mg, Calcium: 25mg, Iron: 1.6mg

Ingredients:
- 1 1/2 cups [135g] chopped cremini mushrooms
- 1/4 cup [40g] chopped red onion
- 1/3 cup [60g] cooked quinoa
- 2 tbsp ground flaxseed
- 1/2 tsp smoked paprika
- 1/4 tsp cayenne pepper
- 1/2 tsp garlic powder
- 1/8 tsp sea salt

Directions:
1. Preheat the air fryer to 375°F [190°C].
2. In a large bowl, combine the chopped cremini mushrooms, onion, cooked quinoa, ground flaxseed, smoked paprika, cayenne pepper, garlic powder, and sea salt.
3. Mix thoroughly until the ingredients bind together and can be formed into firm cubes. Let the mixture sit for 5 minutes to allow the flaxseed to gel.
4. Shape the mixture into 8 compact cubes using your hands or a mold.
5. Arrange the cubes in a single layer in the air fryer basket, leaving space between them.
6. Air fry for 15 minutes, flipping the cubes once halfway through for even crisping.
7. Let the cubes cool for 3 minutes before serving.

Lemon-Garlic Broccoli Bites

⏲ Time: 30 minutes	🍽 Serving Size: 2 servings
🥗 Prep Time: 15 minutes	👨‍🍳 Cook Time: 15 minutes

Each Serving Has:
Calories: 146, Carbohydrates: 14g, Saturated Fat: 1g, Protein: 6g, Fat: 8g, Sodium: 168mg, Potassium: 520mg, Fiber: 5g, Sugar: 3g, Vitamin C: 85mg, Calcium: 65mg, Iron: 1.8mg

Ingredients:
- 1 1/2 cups [135g] chopped broccoli florets
- 1/3 cup [60g] cooked brown rice
- 1/4 cup [20g] chopped yellow onion
- 1 tbsp lemon juice
- 1 tsp lemon zest
- 1 tbsp ground flaxseed
- 1/2 tsp garlic powder
- 1/4 tsp sea salt

Directions:
1. Preheat the air fryer to 375°F [190°C].
2. In a mixing bowl, combine the chopped broccoli florets, cooked brown rice, chopped onion, lemon juice, zest, ground flaxseed, garlic powder, and sea salt.
3. Stir the mixture thoroughly until it holds together; let it sit for 5 minutes to allow the flaxseed to gel and bind.
4. Shape the mixture into 10 small, firm bites using your hands or a scoop.
5. Arrange the bites in a single layer in the air fryer basket, leaving space between them.
6. Cook for 15 minutes, flipping halfway through for even browning.
7. Cool the bites for 5 minutes before serving.

Beet Hummus Air-Fry Chips

- **Time:** 30 minutes
- **Serving Size:** 2 servings
- **Prep Time:** 10 minutes
- **Cook Time:** 20 minutes

Each Serving Has:
Calories: 176, Carbohydrates: 23g, Saturated Fat: 1g, Protein: 5g, Fat: 7g, Sodium: 228mg, Potassium: 410mg, Fiber: 6g, Sugar: 6g, Vitamin C: 5mg, Calcium: 40mg, Iron: 1.3mg

Ingredients:
- 1 medium [150g] peeled raw beet
- 1/4 cup [60g] smooth unsalted hummus
- 1 tbsp lemon juice
- 1/2 tsp ground cumin
- 1/4 tsp smoked paprika
- 1/8 tsp sea salt

Directions:
1. Preheat the air fryer to 350°F [175°C].
2. Using a mandoline or sharp knife, slice the beet into very thin rounds.
3. In a mixing bowl, combine the beet slices with hummus, lemon juice, cumin, smoked paprika, and sea salt. Toss gently to coat each slice evenly.
4. Arrange the coated beet slices in a single layer in the air fryer basket, leaving space between them for airflow.
5. Air fry for 10 minutes, then flip each chip, and cook for another 8–10 minutes, or until crisp and slightly golden on the edges.
6. Let the chips cool for 5 minutes before serving.

Ginger-Oat Mini Discs

- **Time:** 25 minutes
- **Serving Size:** 2 servings
- **Prep Time:** 10 minutes
- **Cook Time:** 15 minutes

Each Serving Has:
Calories: 182, Carbohydrates: 29g, Saturated Fat: 1g, Protein: 5g, Fat: 6g, Sodium: 82mg, Potassium: 190mg, Fiber: 4g, Sugar: 6g, Vitamin C: 0mg, Calcium: 28mg, Iron: 1.7mg

Ingredients:
- 1/2 cup [50g] rolled oats
- 1/4 cup [60g] mashed ripe banana
- 2 tbsp unsweetened applesauce
- 1 tbsp grated fresh ginger
- 1/2 tsp ground cinnamon
- 1/4 tsp ground flaxseed
- 1/8 tsp sea salt

Directions:
1. Preheat the air fryer to 350°F [175°C].
2. In a mixing bowl, combine the oats, mashed banana, applesauce, grated ginger, cinnamon, ground flaxseed, and sea salt. Stir until a thick, sticky mixture forms.
3. Scoop the mixture by heaping tablespoons and shape into flat discs using damp hands.
4. Arrange the discs in a single layer in the air fryer basket, ensuring they don't touch.
5. Air fry for 15 minutes, flipping once halfway through, until golden brown and slightly crisp on the outside.
6. Let the discs cool slightly before serving.

Pumpkin-Crisp Snack Cakes

	Time: 25 minutes		Serving Size: 2 servings
	Prep Time: 10 minutes		Cook Time: 15 minutes

Each Serving Has:
Calories: 188, Carbohydrates: 31g, Saturated Fat: 1g, Protein: 4g, Fat: 5g, Sodium: 92mg, Potassium: 305mg, Fiber: 5g, Sugar: 6g, Vitamin C: 2mg, Calcium: 38mg, Iron: 1.5mg

Ingredients:
- 1/2 cup [120g] unsweetened pumpkin purée
- 1/4 cup [25g] quick oats
- 2 tbsp chopped raw walnuts
- 2 tbsp ground flaxseed
- 1 tbsp unsweetened applesauce
- 1/2 tsp ground cinnamon
- 1/4 tsp ground nutmeg
- 1/8 tsp sea salt

Directions:
1. Preheat the air fryer to 360°F [182°C].
2. In a medium bowl, combine the pumpkin purée, quick oats, chopped walnuts, ground flaxseed, applesauce, cinnamon, nutmeg, and sea salt. Stir thoroughly until a thick, cohesive mixture forms.
3. Shape the mixture into 4 small round cakes, pressing gently to form uniform discs about 1/2 inch thick.
4. Arrange the cakes in a single layer in the air fryer basket, ensuring they are not touching.
5. Air fry for 15 minutes, flipping halfway through, until the edges are crisp and golden.
6. Let the cakes cool for 2 minutes before serving.

Maple Carrot Oat Crunch

	Time: 25 minutes		Serving Size: 2 servings
	Prep Time: 10 minutes		Cook Time: 15 minutes

Each Serving Has:
Calories: 196, Carbohydrates: 32g, Saturated Fat: 1g, Protein: 4g, Fat: 6g, Sodium: 78mg, Potassium: 310mg, Fiber: 5g, Sugar: 9g, Vitamin C: 2mg, Calcium: 42mg, Iron: 1.3mg

Ingredients:
- 1/2 cup [50g] rolled oats
- 1/2 cup [60g] grated carrot
- 2 tbsp chopped raw pecans
- 1 tbsp unsweetened applesauce
- 1 tbsp maple syrup
- 1 tbsp ground flaxseed
- 1/2 tsp ground cinnamon
- 1/4 tsp ground ginger
- 1/8 tsp sea salt

Directions:
1. Preheat the air fryer to 350°F [175°C].
2. In a medium bowl, combine the oats, grated carrot, chopped pecans, applesauce, maple syrup, ground flaxseed, cinnamon, ginger, and sea salt. Mix until evenly incorporated and slightly sticky.
3. Press the mixture into a compact rectangle on a piece of parchment paper, about 1/2 inch thick, then cut into 4 even bars.
4. Gently lift and place the bars in the air fryer basket in a single layer.
5. Air fry for 15 minutes, flipping the bars carefully halfway through, until they are golden and slightly crisp on the edges.
6. Let the crunch cool for 5 minutes before serving.

Seaweed & Rice Crumble Squares

- **Time:** 30 minutes
- **Serving Size:** 2 servings
- **Prep Time:** 10 minutes
- **Cook Time:** 20 minutes

Each Serving Has:
Calories: 192, Carbohydrates: 28g, Saturated Fat: 1g, Protein: 4g, Fat: 6g, Sodium: 228mg, Potassium: 150mg, Fiber: 3g, Sugar: 1g, Vitamin C: 2mg, Calcium: 35mg, Iron: 1.1mg

Ingredients:
- 1 cup [160g] cooked short-grain brown rice, cooled
- 1/4 cup [30g] grated carrot
- 2 tbsp chopped toasted nori sheets
- 1 tbsp ground flaxseed
- 1 tbsp tahini
- 1 tsp low-sodium tamari
- 1/4 tsp garlic powder
- 1/4 tsp smoked paprika

Directions:
1. Preheat the air fryer to 350°F [175°C].
2. In a large bowl, combine the cooked brown rice, grated carrot, chopped nori, ground flaxseed, tahini, tamari, garlic powder, and smoked paprika. Mix thoroughly until the mixture becomes cohesive and sticky.
3. Transfer the mixture to a parchment-lined surface and press it into a 1/2-inch thick rectangle. Cut into 4 equal squares.
4. Carefully place the squares in the air fryer basket in a single layer.
5. Air fry for 10 minutes, then flip gently and cook for an additional 10 minutes, or until the edges are crisp and golden brown.
6. Let the squares cool for 5 minutes before serving.

Crunchy Cucumber Tofu Rolls

- **Time:** 30 minutes
- **Serving Size:** 2 servings
- **Prep Time:** 15 minutes
- **Cook Time:** 15 minutes

Each Serving Has:
Calories: 212, Carbohydrates: 9g, Saturated Fat: 1g, Protein: 14g, Fat: 14g, Sodium: 202mg, Potassium: 335mg, Fiber: 2g, Sugar: 2g, Vitamin C: 6mg, Calcium: 225mg, Iron: 2mg

Ingredients:
- 1 block [200g] extra-firm tofu, pressed and cut into thin rectangular strips
- 1/2 cup [50g] grated cucumber, squeezed to remove excess moisture
- 2 tbsp chopped fresh cilantro
- 1 tbsp tahini
- 1 tsp low-sodium tamari
- 1/4 tsp garlic powder
- 1/8 tsp black pepper
- 1 tsp olive oil
- 8 sheets rice paper, softened

Directions:
1. Preheat the air fryer to 375°F [190°C].
2. In a small bowl, combine the grated cucumber, chopped cilantro, tahini, tamari, garlic powder, and black pepper to form a thick filling paste.
3. Lay out one softened rice paper sheet on a flat surface. Place a strip of tofu horizontally near the bottom, then spread one tablespoon of the cucumber mixture over it. Roll up tightly like a spring roll, folding in the sides as you go. Repeat this process with the remaining ingredients to form 8 rolls.
4. Lightly brush each roll with the olive oil.
5. Arrange rolls in a single layer in the air fryer basket.
6. Air fry for 15 minutes, flipping halfway through, until golden and crisp on all sides.
7. Let the rolls cool slightly before serving.

CHAPTER 3: SNACKS ◊ 39

Spiced Lentil Bites with Dill

- **Time:** 30 minutes
- **Serving Size:** 2 servings
- **Prep Time:** 15 minutes
- **Cook Time:** 15 minutes

Each Serving Has:
Calories: 218, Carbohydrates: 28g, Saturated Fat: 0.5g, Protein: 12g, Fat: 5g, Sodium: 188mg, Potassium: 472mg, Fiber: 10g, Sugar: 3g, Vitamin C: 5mg, Calcium: 48mg, Iron: 3mg

Ingredients:
- 1 cup [170g] cooked green lentils, drained
- 1/4 cup [30g] grated carrot
- 1/4 cup [20g] chopped red onion
- 1 tbsp chopped fresh dill
- 1 tbsp oat flour
- 1 tsp ground cumin
- 1/2 tsp smoked paprika
- 1/8 tsp sea salt
- 1 tsp olive oil

Directions:
1. Preheat the air fryer to 375°F [190°C].
2. In a mixing bowl, combine the cooked lentils, grated carrot, chopped onion, dill, oat flour, cumin, smoked paprika, and sea salt. Mash lightly with a fork to form a cohesive mixture, leaving some lentil texture intact.
3. Shape the mixture into 12 small round bites, pressing gently to hold shape.
4. Brush each bite with olive oil on all sides.
5. Arrange the bites in a single layer in the air fryer basket.
6. Air fry for 15 minutes, flipping halfway through, until golden and slightly crisp on the outside.
7. Remove the bites from the air fryer and serve.

Banana-Almond Air Coins

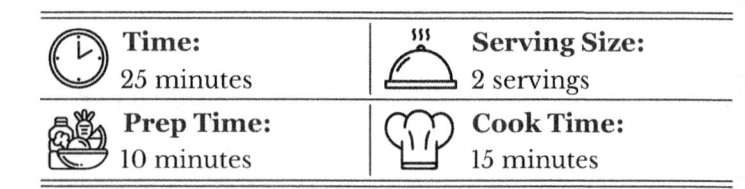

- **Time:** 25 minutes
- **Serving Size:** 2 servings
- **Prep Time:** 10 minutes
- **Cook Time:** 15 minutes

Each Serving Has:
Calories: 212, Carbohydrates: 28g, Saturated Fat: 0.8g, Protein: 5g, Fat: 9g, Sodium: 4mg, Potassium: 376mg, Fiber: 4g, Sugar: 13g, Vitamin C: 6mg, Calcium: 57mg, Iron: 1.2mg

Ingredients:
- 1/2 cup [120g] mashed ripe banana
- 1/3 cup [30g] ground almond flour
- 1/4 cup [20g] rolled oats
- 1/4 tsp ground cinnamon
- 1 tsp chia seeds
- 1 tsp olive oil

Directions:
1. Preheat the air fryer to 350°F [175°C].
2. In a bowl, combine the mashed banana, almond flour, rolled oats, cinnamon, and chia seeds. Mix until a thick, sticky dough forms.
3. Form the mixture into 12 small flat discs, about 1/4 inch thick, and brush the tops lightly with olive oil.
4. Arrange the coins in a single layer in the air fryer basket, ensuring they do not touch each other.
5. Air fry for 15 minutes, flipping once halfway through, until the edges are golden and slightly crisp.
6. Remove the coins from the air fryer and serve.

Avocado & Quinoa Wafers

⏰ Time: 28 minutes	🍽 Serving Size: 2 servings
🥗 Prep Time: 10 minutes	👨‍🍳 Cook Time: 18 minutes

Each Serving Has:
Calories: 218, Carbohydrates: 24g, Saturated Fat: 0.9g, Protein: 6g, Fat: 12g, Sodium: 6mg, Potassium: 486mg, Fiber: 6g, Sugar: 1g, Vitamin C: 9mg, Calcium: 32mg, Iron: 1.6mg

Ingredients:
- 1/2 cup [90g] mashed ripe avocado
- 1/2 cup [85g] cooked and cooled quinoa
- 1/4 cup [20g] rolled oats
- 2 tbsp chopped fresh parsley
- 1/2 tsp ground cumin
- 1 tsp olive oil

Directions:
1. Preheat the air fryer to 375°F [190°C].
2. In a mixing bowl, combine the mashed avocado, cooked quinoa, oats, chopped parsley, and cumin until a thick, cohesive mixture forms.
3. Divide the mixture into 8 equal portions and flatten each into a round wafer, about 1/4 inch thick.
4. Lightly brush the tops of the wafers with olive oil.
5. Arrange the wafers in a single layer in the air fryer basket, ensuring none are overlapping.
6. Air fry for 18 minutes, flipping halfway through, until golden and firm.
7. Remove the wafers from the air fryer and serve.

Chickpea-Cranberry Crisps

⏰ Time: 30 minutes	🍽 Serving Size: 2 servings
🥗 Prep Time: 10 minutes	👨‍🍳 Cook Time: 20 minutes

Each Serving Has:
Calories: 218, Carbohydrates: 28g, Saturated Fat: 0.6g, Protein: 7g, Fat: 7g, Sodium: 46mg, Potassium: 325mg, Fiber: 6g, Sugar: 5g, Vitamin C: 1mg, Calcium: 35mg, Iron: 2.1mg

Ingredients:
- 1/2 cup [90g] mashed cooked chickpeas
- 1/4 cup [25g] rolled oats
- 2 tbsp chopped dried cranberries
- 1 tbsp chopped raw almonds
- 1/2 tsp ground cinnamon
- 1/2 tsp vanilla extract
- 1/2 tbsp olive oil

Directions:
1. Preheat the air fryer to 350°F [175°C].
2. In a medium bowl, combine the mashed chickpeas, oats, chopped cranberries, almonds, cinnamon, and vanilla extract until a sticky, uniform dough forms.
3. Form the dough into 12 small discs, flattening each to about 1/4 inch thick.
4. Lightly brush the tops of the discs with olive oil.
5. Place the discs in a single layer in the air fryer basket, ensuring they do not touch.
6. Air fry for 20 minutes, flipping halfway through, until the edges are crisp and golden.
7. Let the crisps cool for 5 minutes before serving.

Jicama Lime Snack Cubes

⏱ Time: 25 minutes	🍽 Serving Size: 2 servings
🥗 Prep Time: 10 minutes	👨‍🍳 Cook Time: 15 minutes

Each Serving Has:
Calories: 104, Carbohydrates: 23g, Saturated Fat: 0.2g, Protein: 1g, Fat: 1g, Sodium: 72mg, Potassium: 280mg, Fiber: 6g, Sugar: 6g, Vitamin C: 28mg, Calcium: 22mg, Iron: 0.6mg

Ingredients:
- 2 cups [260g] peeled and cubed raw jicama
- 1 tbsp lime juice
- 1 tsp olive oil
- 1/2 tsp chili powder
- 1/4 tsp sea salt

Directions:
1. Preheat the air fryer to 375°F [190°C].
2. In a medium bowl, toss the cubed jicama with lime juice, olive oil, chili powder, and sea salt until evenly coated.
3. Arrange the seasoned jicama cubes in a single layer in the air fryer basket, ensuring they are not overcrowded.
4. Air fry for 15 minutes, shaking the basket halfway through to ensure even cooking and slight crisping.
5. Let the cubes cool for 2 minutes before serving.

Curry-Spiced Sweet Potato Slices

⏱ Time: 25 minutes	🍽 Serving Size: 2 servings
🥗 Prep Time: 10 minutes	👨‍🍳 Cook Time: 15 minutes

Each Serving Has:
Calories: 168, Carbohydrates: 33g, Saturated Fat: 0.4g, Protein: 2g, Fat: 4g, Sodium: 150mg, Potassium: 540mg, Fiber: 5g, Sugar: 7g, Vitamin C: 6mg, Calcium: 44mg, Iron: 1.2mg

Ingredients:
- 2 cups [270g] thinly sliced, peeled sweet potato
- 1 tbsp olive oil
- 1/2 tsp curry powder
- 1/4 tsp ground cumin
- 1/4 tsp sea salt

Directions:
1. Preheat the air fryer to 375°F [190°C].
2. In a large bowl, toss the sweet potato slices with olive oil, curry powder, cumin, and sea salt until evenly coated.
3. Arrange the slices in a single layer in the air fryer basket, working in batches if necessary to avoid overlap.
4. Air fry for 15 minutes, flipping the slices halfway through to promote even browning and crisping.
5. Remove the sweet potato slices from the air fryer and serve.

42 ◊ CHAPTER 3: SNACKS

Roasted Garlic Cauliflower Florets

Time: 25 minutes
Serving Size: 2 servings
Prep Time: 10 minutes
Cook Time: 15 minutes

Each Serving Has:
Calories: 122, Carbohydrates: 11g, Saturated Fat: 0.7g, Protein: 4g, Fat: 7g, Sodium: 170mg, Potassium: 570mg, Fiber: 4g, Sugar: 3g, Vitamin C: 66mg, Calcium: 42mg, Iron: 1.1mg

Ingredients:
- 2 cups [200g] bite-sized cauliflower florets
- 1 tbsp olive oil
- 1 tsp minced garlic
- 1/2 tsp onion powder
- 1/4 tsp sea salt

Directions:
1. Preheat the air fryer to 375°F [190°C].
2. In a mixing bowl, toss the cauliflower florets with olive oil, minced garlic, onion powder, and sea salt until evenly coated.
3. Spread the florets in a single layer in the air fryer basket, ensuring they are not overcrowded.
4. Air fry for 15 minutes, shaking the basket halfway through to promote even roasting.
5. Remove the cauliflower from the air fryer and serve.

Chapter 4: Lunches

Curried Chickpea Air Logs

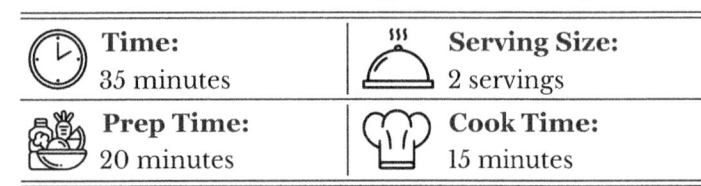

⏰ **Time:** 35 minutes	🍽 **Serving Size:** 2 servings
🥗 **Prep Time:** 20 minutes	👨‍🍳 **Cook Time:** 15 minutes

Each Serving Has:
Calories: 285, Carbohydrates: 34g, Saturated Fat: 0.9g, Protein: 13g, Fat: 8g, Sodium: 420mg, Potassium: 620mg, Fiber: 10g, Sugar: 5g, Vitamin C: 22mg, Calcium: 90mg, Iron: 4.2mg

Ingredients:
- 1 cup [165g] canned chickpeas, rinsed and drained
- 1/4 cup [60g] grated carrot
- 1/4 cup [60g] chopped red bell pepper
- 2 tbsp rolled oats
- 2 tbsp tahini
- 1 tbsp lemon juice
- 1 tbsp ground flaxseed
- 2 tbsp water
- 1 tsp curry powder
- 1/2 tsp ground cumin
- 1/4 tsp smoked paprika
- 1/4 tsp garlic powder
- 1/4 tsp onion powder
- 1/4 tsp sea salt
- 1/8 tsp black pepper

Directions:
1. Preheat the air fryer to 375°F [190°C].
2. In a small bowl, combine the ground flaxseed and water, stirring to form a flax "egg". Let it sit for 5 minutes to thicken.
3. In a mixing bowl, mash the chickpeas using a fork or potato masher until mostly smooth, leaving some chunks for texture.
4. Add the grated carrot, chopped bell pepper, oats, tahini, lemon juice, flax "egg", curry powder, cumin, smoked paprika, garlic powder, onion powder, sea salt, and black pepper to the mashed chickpeas. Mix thoroughly until a cohesive mixture forms.
5. Divide the mixture into four equal portions and shape each portion into a compact log approximately 3 inches [7.5cm] long.
6. Spray the air fryer basket with water or line it with parchment paper to prevent sticking.
7. Arrange the chickpea logs in a single layer in the air fryer basket, ensuring they don't touch.
8. Cook for 15 minutes, flipping the logs halfway through to ensure even browning.
9. Remove the logs from the air fryer and serve.

Air-Fried Falafel Wrap

⏱ Time: 40 minutes	🍽 Serving Size: 2 servings
🥗 Prep Time: 20 minutes	👨‍🍳 Cook Time: 20 minutes

Each Serving Has:
Calories: 318, Carbohydrates: 39g, Saturated Fat: 0.9g, Protein: 11g, Fat: 11g, Sodium: 254mg, Potassium: 541mg, Fiber: 9g, Sugar: 5g, Vitamin C: 15mg, Calcium: 74mg, Iron: 3.1mg

Ingredients:
- 1 cup [165g] cooked chickpeas, rinsed, drained
- 1/4 cup [30g] chopped yellow onion
- 1 tbsp chopped fresh parsley
- 1 tbsp chopped fresh cilantro
- 1 tsp ground cumin
- 1/2 tsp ground coriander
- 1/4 tsp baking powder
- 1 tbsp whole-wheat flour
- 1 tbsp olive oil
- 1/2 cup [45g] thinly sliced red cabbage
- 1/2 cup [60g] grated carrot
- 2 small [50g each] whole-wheat wraps
- 1 tbsp lemon juice

Directions:
1. Preheat the air fryer to 375°F [190°C].
2. In a food processor, combine the cooked chickpeas, chopped onion, parsley, cilantro, cumin, coriander, baking powder, and flour. Pulse until the mixture is coarse and sticks together when pressed.
3. Form the mixture into 8 small falafel balls and brush each with olive oil.
4. Place the falafel balls in a single layer in the air fryer basket. Cook for 10 minutes, then flip and cook for an additional 10 minutes, until golden brown and crisp.
5. Meanwhile, toss the sliced cabbage and grated carrot with lemon juice in a small bowl.
6. Warm the whole-wheat wraps briefly in the air fryer or on a dry skillet.
7. Assemble each wrap with four falafel balls and equal portions of the cabbage-carrot mixture.
8. Roll up the wraps and serve.

Roasted Veggie Stuffed Pita

⏱ Time: 35 minutes	🍽 Serving Size: 2 servings
🥗 Prep Time: 15 minutes	👨‍🍳 Cook Time: 20 minutes

Each Serving Has:
Calories: 328, Carbohydrates: 46g, Saturated Fat: 1.2g, Protein: 9g, Fat: 12g, Sodium: 322mg, Potassium: 588mg, Fiber: 8g, Sugar: 6g, Vitamin C: 48mg, Calcium: 71mg, Iron: 2.6mg

Ingredients:
- 1/2 cup [70g] diced red bell pepper
- 1/2 cup [60g] chopped zucchini
- 1/2 cup [55g] chopped red onion
- 1/2 cup [90g] halved cherry tomatoes
- 1 tbsp olive oil
- 1/2 tsp dried oregano
- 1/4 tsp garlic powder
- 1/4 tsp black pepper
- 2 small [50g each] whole-wheat pita breads
- 1 cup [70g] chopped fresh spinach

Directions:
1. Preheat the air fryer to 375°F [190°C].
2. In a mixing bowl, toss the diced bell pepper, chopped zucchini, onion, and halved cherry tomatoes with olive oil, oregano, garlic powder, and black pepper until evenly coated.
3. Spread the seasoned vegetables in a single layer in the air fryer basket.
4. Cook for 10 minutes, then shake the basket and continue cooking for an additional 10 minutes, until the vegetables are tender and lightly charred on the outside.
5. While the vegetables cook, warm the whole-wheat pita breads in a dry skillet or air fryer for 1–2 minutes.
6. Slice open each pita and stuff with chopped spinach and equal portions of the roasted vegetables, then serve.

CHAPTER 4: LUNCHES ◊ 45

Lentil & Brown Rice Patties

⏰ Time: 35 minutes	🍽 Serving Size: 2 servings
🥫 Prep Time: 15 minutes	👨‍🍳 Cook Time: 20 minutes

Each Serving Has:
Calories: 287, Carbohydrates: 38g, Saturated Fat: 0.8g, Protein: 11g, Fat: 8g, Sodium: 224mg, Potassium: 512mg, Fiber: 9g, Sugar: 2g, Vitamin C: 5mg, Calcium: 42mg, Iron: 2.8mg

Ingredients:
- 1/2 cup [100g] cooked green lentils, drained
- 1/2 cup [95g] cooked brown rice, cooled
- 1/4 cup [30g] chopped red onion
- 1/4 cup [25g] grated carrot
- 2 tbsp chopped fresh parsley
- 1 tbsp ground flaxseed
- 1 tbsp water
- 1/2 tsp garlic powder
- 1/2 tsp smoked paprika
- 1/4 tsp sea salt
- 1 tbsp olive oil

Directions:
1. Preheat the air fryer to 375°F [190°C].
2. In a small bowl, mix the ground flaxseed and water to create a flax "egg". Let it sit for 5 minutes to thicken.
3. In a mixing bowl, combine the cooked lentils, brown rice, chopped onion, grated carrot, parsley, garlic powder, smoked paprika, and sea salt.
4. Add the flax "egg" and mash the contents together using a fork or potato masher until partially smooth with some texture.
5. Divide the mixture into 4 equal portions and shape into patties about 1/2 inch thick.
6. Brush each patty lightly with the olive oil on both sides.
7. Place the patties in a single layer in the air fryer basket.
8. Cook for 10 minutes, then flip gently and cook for an additional 10 minutes, until golden and crisp.
9. Remove the patties from the air fryer and serve.

Thai-Inspired Tofu Lettuce Boats

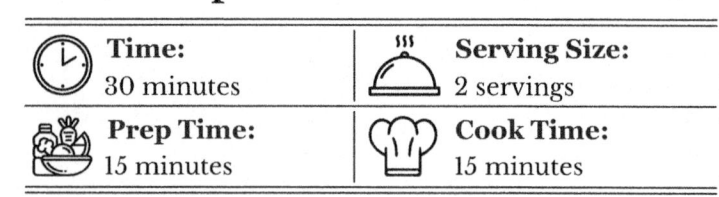

⏰ Time: 30 minutes	🍽 Serving Size: 2 servings
🥫 Prep Time: 15 minutes	👨‍🍳 Cook Time: 15 minutes

Each Serving Has:
Calories: 248, Carbohydrates: 18g, Saturated Fat: 1g, Protein: 14g, Fat: 15g, Sodium: 412mg, Potassium: 642mg, Fiber: 4g, Sugar: 6g, Vitamin C: 27mg, Calcium: 351mg, Iron: 4mg

Ingredients:
- 1 cup [180g] cubed extra-firm tofu, pressed and drained
- 1/2 cup [70g] chopped red bell pepper
- 1/4 cup [25g] grated carrot
- 2 tbsp chopped green onion
- 1 tbsp chopped fresh cilantro
- 1 tbsp lime juice
- 1 tbsp low-sodium soy sauce
- 1/2 tsp grated fresh ginger
- 1/2 tsp garlic powder
- 1 tsp sesame oil
- 4 large crisp butter lettuce leaves

Directions:
1. Preheat the air fryer to 375°F [190°C].
2. In a bowl, combine the cubed tofu, chopped bell pepper, grated carrot, green onion, soy sauce, lime juice, grated ginger, garlic powder, and sesame oil. Toss until evenly coated.
3. Arrange the mixture in a single layer in the air fryer basket.
4. Cook for 15 minutes, shaking the basket halfway through, until the tofu is golden and edges are crisp.
5. Remove the vegetable-tofu mixture from the air fryer and gently fold in the chopped cilantro.
6. Spoon the tofu filling evenly into the butter lettuce leaves and serve.

Air-Fried Mushroom-Spinach Rolls

⏲ Time: 30 minutes	🍽 Serving Size: 2 servings
🥗 Prep Time: 15 minutes	👨‍🍳 Cook Time: 15 minutes

Each Serving Has:
Calories: 224, Carbohydrates: 20g, Saturated Fat: 1g, Protein: 9g, Fat: 11g, Sodium: 290mg, Potassium: 615mg, Fiber: 4g, Sugar: 3g, Vitamin C: 17mg, Calcium: 106mg, Iron: 3mg

Ingredients:
- 1 cup [90g] chopped cremini mushrooms
- 1 cup [30g] loosely packed chopped fresh spinach
- 1/4 cup [30g] diced red onion
- 1/2 tsp garlic powder
- 1/4 tsp black pepper
- 1/8 tsp sea salt
- 1 tbsp olive oil (+ 1/2 tsp extra for brushing)
- 4 sheets rice paper, softened

Directions:
1. Preheat the air fryer to 375°F [190°C].
2. In a skillet over medium heat, sauté the chopped mushrooms, spinach, and diced onion in olive oil for 5–6 minutes, or until the vegetables are softened and most of the moisture has evaporated. Stir in the garlic powder, black pepper, and salt. Let cool for 2 minutes.
3. Lay out softened rice paper sheets on a clean surface.
4. Spoon equal amounts of the mushroom-spinach filling onto the bottom third of each sheet. Fold the sides inward, then roll tightly to form compact rolls.
5. Lightly brush the air fryer basket with olive oil. Arrange the rolls in a single layer.
6. Air-fry for 10–12 minutes, flipping the rolls once halfway through, until they are golden and crisp on the outside.
7. Remove the rolls from the air fryer and serve.

Sweet Potato Chickpea Pockets

⏲ Time: 35 minutes	🍽 Serving Size: 2 servings
🥗 Prep Time: 15 minutes	👨‍🍳 Cook Time: 20 minutes

Each Serving Has:
Calories: 286, Carbohydrates: 38g, Saturated Fat: 1g, Protein: 9g, Fat: 10g, Sodium: 250mg, Potassium: 640mg, Fiber: 8g, Sugar: 6g, Vitamin C: 17mg, Calcium: 74mg, Iron: 3mg

Ingredients:
- 1 cup [200g] mashed cooked sweet potato
- 1/2 cup [85g] mashed cooked chickpeas, rinsed, drained
- 1/4 cup [30g] chopped red onion
- 1/2 tsp ground cumin
- 1/4 tsp smoked paprika
- 1/8 tsp sea salt
- 1 tbsp olive oil (+ 1/2 tsp extra for brushing)
- 2 whole-grain pita pockets, halved

Directions:
1. Preheat the air fryer to 375°F [190°C].
2. In a mixing bowl, combine the mashed sweet potato, chickpeas, chopped onion, cumin, smoked paprika, sea salt, and olive oil. Stir until well combined and the mixture holds its shape.
3. Carefully open the halved pita pockets and fill each half with the sweet potato-chickpea mixture, pressing the filling in gently to form a compact pocket.
4. Lightly brush the air fryer basket with oil. Arrange the filled pita halves in a single layer.
5. Air-fry for 10 minutes. Flip and continue cooking for 8–10 minutes, or until the pita is crisp and golden.
6. Remove the chickpea pockets from the air fryer and serve.

CHAPTER 4: LUNCHES

Crispy Quinoa Salad Bites

🕐 Time: 30 minutes	🍽 Serving Size: 2 servings
🥗 Prep Time: 15 minutes	👨‍🍳 Cook Time: 15 minutes

Each Serving Has:
Calories: 248, Carbohydrates: 32g, Saturated Fat: 1g, Protein: 8g, Fat: 9g, Sodium: 214mg, Potassium: 480mg, Fiber: 6g, Sugar: 3g, Vitamin C: 18mg, Calcium: 54mg, Iron: 3mg

Ingredients:
- 1 cup [170g] cooked quinoa, cooled
- 1/2 cup [100g] grated carrot
- 1/2 cup [80g] chopped cucumber
- 1/4 cup [40g] chopped red bell pepper
- 1 tbsp chopped fresh parsley
- 1 tbsp olive oil (+ 1/2 tsp extra for brushing)
- 1/2 tsp garlic powder
- 1/4 tsp ground cumin
- 1/8 tsp sea salt

Directions:
1. Preheat the air fryer to 375°F [190°C].
2. In a large bowl, combine the cooked quinoa, grated carrot, chopped cucumber, bell pepper, and parsley.
3. Sprinkle in the garlic powder, cumin, sea salt, and drizzle with olive oil. Mix thoroughly until the ingredients hold together when pressed.
4. Scoop the mixture into 8 equal portions and form into small patties using your hands.
5. Lightly brush the air fryer basket with the olive oil. Place the patties in a single layer, leaving space between each.
6. Air-fry for 7 minutes. Flip gently and cook for an additional 6–8 minutes, or until golden and crisp on both sides.
7. Remove the bites from the air fryer and serve.

Zucchini-Carrot Fritter Sandwich

🕐 Time: 35 minutes	🍽 Serving Size: 2 servings
🥗 Prep Time: 20 minutes	👨‍🍳 Cook Time: 15 minutes

Each Serving Has:
Calories: 298, Carbohydrates: 36g, Saturated Fat: 1g, Protein: 8g, Fat: 13g, Sodium: 312mg, Potassium: 754mg, Fiber: 7g, Sugar: 9g, Vitamin C: 22mg, Calcium: 72mg, Iron: 3mg

Ingredients:
- 1 cup [120g] grated zucchini, excess moisture squeezed out
- 1/2 cup [60g] grated carrot
- 1/4 cup [25g] chopped red onion
- 1/4 cup [20g] rolled oats
- 1 tbsp ground flaxseed
- 2 tbsp water
- 1 tbsp olive oil (+ 1/2 tsp extra for brushing)
- 1/2 tsp ground cumin
- 1/4 tsp smoked paprika
- 2 whole-grain sandwich buns
- 1 cup [40g] shredded lettuce

Directions:
1. Preheat the air fryer to 375°F [190°C].
2. In a small bowl, mix the ground flaxseed and water to create a flax "egg". Let it sit for 5 minutes to thicken.
3. In a medium bowl, combine the grated zucchini, carrot, chopped onion, oats, flax "egg", olive oil, cumin, and smoked paprika. Mix thoroughly until a sticky mixture forms.
4. Divide the mixture into 4 equal portions and shape each into a small patty.
5. Brush the air fryer basket with olive oil. Arrange the patties in a single layer without overlapping.
6. Air-fry for 15 minutes, flipping halfway through, until golden brown and crisp on the edges.
7. Slice the buns and layer each bottom half with shredded lettuce.
8. Tuck two fritters into each bun and cover with the top half, then serve.

Eggplant-Bulgur Medallions

- **Time:** 40 minutes
- **Serving Size:** 2 servings
- **Prep Time:** 20 minutes
- **Cook Time:** 20 minutes

Each Serving Has:
Calories: 246, Carbohydrates: 33g, Saturated Fat: 1g, Protein: 6g, Fat: 9g, Sodium: 180mg, Potassium: 538mg, Fiber: 8g, Sugar: 8g, Vitamin C: 6mg, Calcium: 28mg, Iron: 2mg

Ingredients:
- 1 cup [150g] chopped eggplant
- 1/2 cup [95g] cooked medium-grain bulgur
- 1/4 cup [30g] grated carrot
- 2 tbsp chopped red onion
- 1 tbsp ground flaxseed
- 2 tbsp water
- 1 tbsp olive oil (+ 1/2 tsp extra for brushing)
- 1/2 tsp garlic powder
- 1/4 tsp sea salt

Directions:
1. Preheat the air fryer to 375°F [190°C].
2. In a small bowl, mix the ground flaxseed and water to create a flax "egg". Let it sit for 5 minutes to thicken.
3. In a skillet over medium heat, cook the chopped eggplant in 1 teaspoon of olive oil for 5–6 minutes, stirring occasionally, until tender. Remove from heat and cool slightly.
4. In a mixing bowl, combine the cooked eggplant, bulgur, grated carrot, chopped onion, flax "egg", remaining olive oil, garlic powder, and sea salt. Mix until well combined.
5. Shape the mixture into 4 round medallions, pressing firmly to help them hold together.
6. Brush the air fryer basket with olive oil and arrange the medallions in a single layer, ensuring they do not overlap.
7. Air-fry for 18–20 minutes, flipping halfway through, until golden and crisp on both sides.
8. Remove the medallions from the air fryer and serve.

Tofu Kale Crunch Wrap

- **Time:** 35 minutes
- **Serving Size:** 2 servings
- **Prep Time:** 20 minutes
- **Cook Time:** 15 minutes

Each Serving Has:
Calories: 294, Carbohydrates: 27g, Saturated Fat: 1g, Protein: 15g, Fat: 14g, Sodium: 300mg, Potassium: 562mg, Fiber: 5g, Sugar: 3g, Vitamin C: 37mg, Calcium: 276mg, Iron: 3mg

Ingredients:
- 1 cup [150g] diced firm tofu, pressed
- 1/2 cup [75g] chopped kale, stems removed
- 1/4 cup [40g] grated carrot
- 2 tbsp chopped red onion
- 1 tbsp olive oil
- 1/2 tsp smoked paprika
- 1/4 tsp garlic powder
- 1/4 tsp sea salt
- 2 medium [60g each] whole-grain tortillas

Directions:
1. Preheat the air fryer to 375°F [190°C].
2. In a bowl, toss the diced tofu with olive oil, smoked paprika, garlic powder, and sea salt until evenly coated.
3. Place the tofu in the air fryer basket in a single layer. Air-fry for 12 minutes, shaking the basket halfway through for even browning.
4. While the tofu cooks, combine the chopped kale, onion, and grated carrot in a separate bowl. Gently massage the kale with your hands to soften it.
5. Once the tofu is done, add it to the kale mixture and toss to combine.
6. Lay out the whole-grain tortillas and evenly distribute the tofu-kale mixture across the center of each.
7. Fold the sides and roll tightly to form wraps.
8. Place the wraps seam-side down in the air fryer basket and air-fry for 3 minutes to crisp the exterior.
9. Remove the wraps from the air fryer and serve.

Smoky Black Bean Air Cakes

⏲ Time: 35 minutes	🍽 Serving Size: 2 servings
🥗 Prep Time: 20 minutes	👨‍🍳 Cook Time: 15 minutes

Each Serving Has:
Calories: 252, Carbohydrates: 30g, Saturated Fat: 0.8g, Protein: 12g, Fat: 8g, Sodium: 290mg, Potassium: 614mg, Fiber: 9g, Sugar: 2g, Vitamin C: 16mg, Calcium: 86mg, Iron: 3mg

Ingredients:
- 3/4 cup [130g] mashed cooked black beans
- 1/2 cup [85g] chopped red bell pepper
- 1/4 cup [40g] diced red onion
- 1/4 cup [25g] rolled oats
- 1 tbsp ground flaxseed
- 1 tbsp water
- 1 tbsp olive oil
- 1/2 tsp smoked paprika
- 1/4 tsp ground cumin
- 1/4 tsp sea salt

Directions:
1. Preheat the air fryer to 375°F [190°C].
2. In a small bowl, mix the ground flaxseed and water to create a flax "egg". Let it sit for 5 minutes to thicken.
3. In a large bowl, combine the mashed black beans, chopped bell pepper, diced onion, oats, olive oil, smoked paprika, cumin, sea salt, and the prepared flax "egg".
4. Mix thoroughly until the mixture holds together when pressed.
5. Form the mixture into 4 small patties of equal size.
6. Place the patties in the air fryer basket in a single layer.
7. Air-fry for 15 minutes, flipping halfway through, until the cakes are crisp and golden on the outside.
8. Remove the cakes from the air fryer and serve.

Roasted Red Pepper & Hummus Wrap

⏲ Time: 30 minutes	🍽 Serving Size: 2 servings
🥗 Prep Time: 15 minutes	👨‍🍳 Cook Time: 15 minutes

Each Serving Has:
Calories: 314, Carbohydrates: 38g, Saturated Fat: 1g, Protein: 9g, Fat: 14g, Sodium: 412mg, Potassium: 492mg, Fiber: 8g, Sugar: 6g, Vitamin C: 74mg, Calcium: 56mg, Iron: 2mg

Ingredients:
- 1 cup [150g] sliced red bell pepper
- 1/2 cup [90g] thinly sliced zucchini
- 1 tbsp olive oil
- 1/2 tsp smoked paprika
- 1/4 tsp sea salt
- 1/4 tsp black pepper
- 1/2 cup [120g] plain hummus
- 2 large [100g each] whole-grain wraps
- 1 cup [30g] shredded romaine lettuce

Directions:
1. Preheat the air fryer to 375°F [190°C].
2. In a bowl, toss the sliced bell pepper and zucchini with olive oil, smoked paprika, sea salt, and black pepper until evenly coated.
3. Arrange the vegetables in a single layer in the air fryer basket.
4. Cook for 12–15 minutes, shaking the basket once halfway through, until vegetables are tender and slightly charred.
5. Lay the whole-grain wraps flat and spread hummus evenly across the center of each.
6. Top the hummus with equal portions of the air-fried vegetables and shredded romaine lettuce.
7. Roll each wrap tightly, tucking in the ends as you go.
8. Slice in half and serve.

Tomato-Lentil Crunch Sliders

⏰ Time: 35 minutes	🍽 Serving Size: 2 servings
🥗 Prep Time: 20 minutes	👨‍🍳 Cook Time: 15 minutes

Each Serving Has:
Calories: 298, Carbohydrates: 34g, Saturated Fat: 0.8g, Protein: 12g, Fat: 9g, Sodium: 292mg, Potassium: 746mg, Fiber: 9g, Sugar: 5g, Vitamin C: 18mg, Calcium: 54mg, Iron: 4mg

Ingredients:
- 1/2 cup [100g] cooked green lentils, drained
- 1/2 cup [80g] grated zucchini
- 1/2 cup [80g] chopped ripe tomato
- 1/4 cup [40g] chopped red onion
- 1/4 cup [25g] quick oats
- 1 tbsp ground flaxseed
- 1 tbsp olive oil
- 1/2 tsp garlic powder
- 1/2 tsp smoked paprika
- 1/4 tsp sea salt
- 2 small [50g each] whole-grain slider buns
- 1/2 cup [15g] shredded romaine lettuce

Directions:
1. Preheat the air fryer to 375°F [190°C].
2. In a mixing bowl, combine the cooked lentils, grated zucchini, chopped tomato, onion, quick oats, ground flaxseed, garlic powder, smoked paprika, sea salt, and olive oil.
3. Mash the mixture lightly with a fork, just enough to help bind the ingredients, while keeping some texture.
4. Form the mixture into 4 small patties of equal size and thickness.
5. Arrange the patties in a single layer in the air fryer basket.
6. Cook for 14–15 minutes, flipping once halfway through, until golden and crisp on both sides.
7. Slice the slider buns and layer each bottom half with romaine lettuce and two patties.
8. Cover with the top buns and serve.

Chickpea-Cauliflower Air Balls

⏰ Time: 30 minutes	🍽 Serving Size: 2 servings
🥗 Prep Time: 15 minutes	👨‍🍳 Cook Time: 15 minutes

Each Serving Has:
Calories: 236, Carbohydrates: 30g, Saturated Fat: 0.6g, Protein: 10g, Fat: 7g, Sodium: 290mg, Potassium: 680mg, Fiber: 8g, Sugar: 5g, Vitamin C: 56mg, Calcium: 68mg, Iron: 3mg

Ingredients:
- 1 cup [165g] cooked chickpeas, rinsed, drained
- 1 cup [100g] chopped cauliflower florets
- 1/4 cup [30g] chopped red onion
- 2 tbsp chopped fresh parsley
- 2 tbsp quick oats
- 1 tbsp olive oil
- 1/2 tsp ground cumin
- 1/4 tsp garlic powder
- 1/4 tsp smoked paprika
- 1/4 tsp sea salt

Directions:
1. Preheat the air fryer to 375°F [190°C].
2. In a large bowl, combine the chickpeas, chopped cauliflower, onion, parsley, quick oats, olive oil, cumin, garlic powder, smoked paprika, and sea salt.
3. Mash the mixture using a fork or potato masher until most of the chickpeas and cauliflower are broken down and the mixture holds together.
4. Shape the mixture into 6 evenly sized balls.
5. Place the balls in the air fryer basket in a single layer.
6. Air-fry for 15 minutes, shaking the basket once halfway through, until golden and slightly crisp on the outside.
7. Remove the balls from the air fryer and serve.

Broccoli-Sweet Potato Pocket

Time: 30 minutes	Serving Size: 2 servings
Prep Time: 15 minutes	Cook Time: 15 minutes

Each Serving Has:
Calories: 248, Carbohydrates: 37g, Saturated Fat: 0.9g, Protein: 7g, Fat: 6g, Sodium: 260mg, Potassium: 730mg, Fiber: 8g, Sugar: 7g, Vitamin C: 74mg, Calcium: 72mg, Iron: 2.5mg

Ingredients:
- 1 cup [130g] chopped steamed broccoli florets
- 3/4 cup [150g] mashed cooked sweet potato
- 1/4 cup [30g] chopped red onion
- 1/4 cup [20g] quick oats
- 2 tbsp chopped fresh parsley
- 1/2 tsp ground cumin
- 1/4 tsp garlic powder
- 1/4 tsp sea salt
- 1 tbsp olive oil
- 2 medium whole-grain pita breads

Directions:
1. Preheat the air fryer to 375°F [190°C].
2. In a mixing bowl, combine the chopped broccoli florets, mashed sweet potato, onion, quick oats, parsley, cumin, garlic powder, sea salt, and olive oil. Stir until the mixture is well combined and holds together.
3. Carefully cut each pita bread in half to form two pockets, then gently open the pockets.
4. Divide the mixture into four equal parts and stuff each pita half evenly, pressing the filling in firmly.
5. Place the stuffed pockets in the air fryer basket in a single layer.
6. Cook for 15 minutes, flipping once halfway through, until the edges are lightly crisp and the filling is heated through.
7. Remove the stuffed pockets from the air fryer and serve.

Millet-Lime Veggie Boats

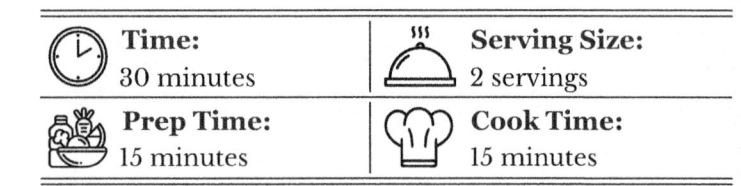

Time: 30 minutes	Serving Size: 2 servings
Prep Time: 15 minutes	Cook Time: 15 minutes

Each Serving Has:
Calories: 258, Carbohydrates: 42g, Saturated Fat: 0.8g, Protein: 6g, Fat: 7g, Sodium: 240mg, Potassium: 620mg, Fiber: 7g, Sugar: 5g, Vitamin C: 51mg, Calcium: 68mg, Iron: 2.3mg

Ingredients:
- 2 medium bell peppers, halved and seeds removed
- 1/2 cup [95g] cooked millet
- 1/2 cup [80g] chopped zucchini
- 1/4 cup [40g] chopped tomato
- 1/4 cup [30g] grated carrot
- 1 tbsp chopped fresh cilantro
- 1 tbsp lime juice
- 1/2 tsp ground cumin
- 1/4 tsp garlic powder
- 1/8 tsp sea salt
- 1 tbsp olive oil

Directions:
1. Preheat the air fryer to 375°F [190°C].
2. In a mixing bowl, combine the cooked millet, chopped zucchini, tomato, grated carrot, cilantro, lime juice, cumin, garlic powder, sea salt, and olive oil. Mix until fully incorporated.
3. Stuff each bell pepper half evenly with the millet mixture, gently pressing the filling in.
4. Place the stuffed pepper halves in the air fryer basket in a single layer.
5. Air fry for 15 minutes, or until the peppers are tender and the tops are lightly golden.
6. Remove the bell peppers from the air fryer and serve warm.

Crunchy Parsnip Wraps

⏰ Time: 30 minutes	🍽 Serving Size: 2 servings
🥗 Prep Time: 15 minutes	👨‍🍳 Cook Time: 15 minutes

Each Serving Has:
Calories: 248, Carbohydrates: 35g, Saturated Fat: 0.9g, Protein: 5g, Fat: 8g, Sodium: 310mg, Potassium: 580mg, Fiber: 7g, Sugar: 9g, Vitamin C: 29mg, Calcium: 58mg, Iron: 2.1mg

Ingredients:
- 1 cup [130g] grated parsnip
- 1/2 cup [80g] chopped red bell pepper
- 1/4 cup [25g] chopped red onion
- 1 tbsp chopped fresh parsley
- 1/2 tsp ground coriander
- 1/4 tsp smoked paprika
- 1/8 tsp sea salt
- 1 tbsp olive oil
- 2 large whole-grain tortillas

Directions:
1. Preheat the air fryer to 375°F [190°C].
2. In a bowl, combine the grated parsnip, chopped bell pepper, onion, parsley, coriander, smoked paprika, sea salt, and olive oil. Mix until evenly coated.
3. Divide the mixture evenly between the tortillas and roll each into a tight wrap.
4. Place the wraps seam-side down in the air fryer basket.
5. Air fry for 12–15 minutes, flipping the wraps once halfway through, until they are golden and crisp on both sides.
6. Remove the wraps from the air fryer and serve.

Carrot-Lentil Air Burgers

⏰ Time: 35 minutes	🍽 Serving Size: 2 servings
🥗 Prep Time: 20 minutes	👨‍🍳 Cook Time: 15 minutes

Each Serving Has:
Calories: 256, Carbohydrates: 35g, Saturated Fat: 0.8g, Protein: 10g, Fat: 7g, Sodium: 310mg, Potassium: 690mg, Fiber: 9g, Sugar: 5g, Vitamin C: 10mg, Calcium: 48mg, Iron: 3.3mg

Ingredients:
- 1/2 cup [100g] mashed cooked lentils
- 1/2 cup [60g] grated carrot
- 1/4 cup [35g] chopped yellow onion
- 1/4 cup [30g] oat flour
- 1 tbsp chopped fresh parsley
- 1 tbsp olive oil (+ 1/2 tsp for brushing)
- 1/2 tsp ground cumin
- 1/4 tsp garlic powder
- 1/8 tsp sea salt

Directions:
1. Preheat the air fryer to 375°F [190°C].
2. In a mixing bowl, combine the mashed lentils, grated carrot, chopped onion, oat flour, parsley, cumin, garlic powder, sea salt, and olive oil. Mix well until the mixture binds.
3. Shape the mixture into two equal-sized burger patties.
4. Brush the air fryer basket with oil. Place the patties in a single layer.
5. Cook for 15 minutes, flipping the burgers halfway through, until they are golden and firm.
6. Remove the patties from the air fryer and serve warm.

CHAPTER 4: LUNCHES

Cucumber Quinoa Salad Wrap

Time: 25 minutes	Serving Size: 2 servings
Prep Time: 15 minutes	Cook Time: 10 minutes

Each Serving Has:
Calories: 286, Carbohydrates: 37g, Saturated Fat: 1g, Protein: 8g, Fat: 10g, Sodium: 260mg, Potassium: 580mg, Fiber: 6g, Sugar: 4g, Vitamin C: 12mg, Calcium: 45mg, Iron: 2.5mg

Ingredients:
- 1/2 cup [95g] cooked quinoa, cooled
- 1/2 cup [70g] chopped cucumber
- 1/4 cup [30g] grated carrot
- 1/4 cup [35g] chopped red bell pepper
- 1 tbsp chopped fresh mint
- 1 tbsp olive oil
- 1 tsp lime juice
- 1/8 tsp sea salt
- 2 large whole-grain tortillas

Directions:
1. Preheat the air fryer to 375°F [190°C].
2. In a mixing bowl, combine the cooked quinoa, chopped cucumber, grated carrot, bell pepper, mint, olive oil, lime juice, and sea salt. Stir until evenly mixed.
3. Lay out the tortillas and spoon the quinoa salad evenly down the center of each. Roll each into a wrap, folding in the edges to seal.
4. Place the wraps seam side down in the air fryer basket.
5. Cook for 10 minutes, flipping the wraps once halfway through, until the outside is lightly crisped.
6. Remove the wraps from the air fryer, slice, and serve warm.

Spicy Edamame Lettuce Cups

Time: 25 minutes	Serving Size: 2 servings
Prep Time: 10 minutes	Cook Time: 15 minutes

Each Serving Has:
Calories: 260, Carbohydrates: 22g, Saturated Fat: 1g, Protein: 13g, Fat: 11g, Sodium: 290mg, Potassium: 610mg, Fiber: 7g, Sugar: 4g, Vitamin C: 22mg, Calcium: 80mg, Iron: 3.1mg

Ingredients:
- 1 cup [150g] shelled edamame, thawed if frozen
- 1/2 cup [75g] chopped red bell pepper
- 1/4 cup [30g] grated carrot
- 1 tbsp chopped fresh cilantro
- 1 tbsp olive oil
- 1/2 tsp garlic powder
- 1/4 tsp smoked paprika
- 1/8 tsp cayenne pepper
- 1/8 tsp sea salt
- 4 large leaves butter lettuce

Directions:
1. Preheat the air fryer to 375°F [190°C].
2. In a bowl, combine the edamame, chopped bell pepper, grated carrot, cilantro, olive oil, garlic powder, smoked paprika, cayenne pepper, and sea salt. Mix until vegetables are evenly coated with seasoning.
3. Spread the mixture in a single layer in the air fryer basket.
4. Cook for 15 minutes, shaking the basket halfway through to ensure even crisping.
5. Spoon the roasted spicy edamame mixture into the butter lettuce leaves and serve warm.

Green Bean & Rice Cakes

Time: 30 minutes
Serving Size: 2 servings
Prep Time: 10 minutes
Cook Time: 20 minutes

Each Serving Has:
Calories: 230, Carbohydrates: 34g, Saturated Fat: 1g, Protein: 8g, Fat: 7g, Sodium: 260mg, Potassium: 430mg, Fiber: 5g, Sugar: 3g, Vitamin C: 22mg, Calcium: 70mg, Iron: 2.8mg

Ingredients:
- 1 cup [150g] chopped green beans, steamed
- 1 cup [200g] cooked brown rice
- 1/4 cup [30g] grated carrot
- 1/4 cup [15g] chopped fresh parsley
- 2 tbsp whole-wheat flour
- 1 tbsp olive oil
- 1/2 tsp garlic powder
- 1/4 tsp ground cumin
- 1/4 tsp sea salt
- 1/8 tsp black pepper

Directions:
1. Preheat the air fryer to 375°F [190°C].
2. In a mixing bowl, combine the chopped beans, cooked brown rice, grated carrot, chopped parsley, flour, olive oil, garlic powder, cumin, sea salt, and black pepper. Mix until the mixture holds together when pressed.
3. Divide the mixture evenly and form into 4 compact cakes.
4. Arrange the cakes in a single layer in the air fryer basket.
5. Cook for 20 minutes, flipping the cakes carefully at the halfway mark for even crisping.
6. Remove the cakes from the air fryer and serve warm.

Herbed Zucchini Tofu Discs

Time: 30 minutes
Serving Size: 2 servings
Prep Time: 10 minutes
Cook Time: 20 minutes

Each Serving Has:
Calories: 215, Carbohydrates: 12g, Saturated Fat: 1g, Protein: 14g, Fat: 14g, Sodium: 340mg, Potassium: 520mg, Fiber: 4g, Sugar: 3g, Vitamin C: 22mg, Calcium: 310mg, Iron: 3.2mg

Ingredients:
- 1 cup [150g] grated zucchini, excess moisture squeezed out
- 1 cup [200g] firm tofu, mashed
- 1/4 cup [30g] chopped red bell pepper
- 2 tbsp chopped fresh parsley
- 1 tbsp nutritional yeast
- 1 tbsp olive oil
- 1/2 tsp garlic powder
- 1/2 tsp dried oregano
- 1/4 tsp smoked paprika
- 1/4 tsp sea salt
- 1/8 tsp black pepper

Directions:
1. Preheat the air fryer to 375°F [190°C].
2. In a mixing bowl, combine the grated zucchini, mashed tofu, chopped bell pepper, parsley, nutritional yeast, olive oil, garlic powder, oregano, smoked paprika, sea salt, and black pepper. Mix thoroughly until a uniform mixture forms.
3. Divide the mixture into 8 equal portions and shape each portion into flat, round discs about 2 inches [5 cm] in diameter.
4. Arrange the discs in a single layer in the air fryer basket, ensuring they do not overlap.
5. Cook for 20 minutes, flipping the discs carefully at the halfway point for even crisping.
6. Remove the discs from the air fryer and serve.

BBQ Cauliflower Pita Pockets

🕐 Time: 30 minutes	🍽 Serving Size: 2 servings
🥗 Prep Time: 10 minutes	👨‍🍳 Cook Time: 20 minutes

Each Serving Has:
Calories: 320, Carbohydrates: 42g, Saturated Fat: 1g, Protein: 10g, Fat: 11g, Sodium: 540mg, Potassium: 680mg, Fiber: 8g, Sugar: 9g, Vitamin C: 75mg, Calcium: 140mg, Iron: 3.5mg

Ingredients:
- 2 cups [200g] cauliflower florets
- 1/2 cup [120ml] low-sodium BBQ sauce
- 1 tbsp olive oil
- 1/2 tsp smoked paprika
- 1/4 tsp garlic powder
- 1/4 tsp onion powder
- 1/4 tsp black pepper
- 2 whole-grain pita pockets
- 1 cup [50g] shredded romaine lettuce
- 1/2 cup [75g] thinly sliced cucumber
- 1/4 cup [30g] chopped red onion
- 1 tbsp chopped fresh cilantro

Directions:
1. Preheat the air fryer to 375°F [190°C].
2. In a mixing bowl, toss the cauliflower florets with olive oil, smoked paprika, garlic powder, onion powder, and black pepper until evenly coated.
3. Arrange the seasoned cauliflower florets in a single layer in the air fryer basket.
4. Cook for 15 minutes, shaking the basket halfway through for even cooking.
5. Transfer the cooked cauliflower back to the mixing bowl and toss it with the BBQ sauce until it is fully coated.
6. Return the cauliflower to the air fryer and cook for an additional 5 minutes to slightly caramelize the sauce.
7. While the cauliflower is finishing, warm the pita pockets, if desired.
8. Fill each pita pocket with the shredded romaine lettuce, sliced cucumber, chopped onion, and the BBQ cauliflower, then serve.

Garlic Sweet Corn Cakes

🕐 Time: 30 minutes	🍽 Serving Size: 2 servings
🥗 Prep Time: 10 minutes	👨‍🍳 Cook Time: 20 minutes

Each Serving Has:
Calories: 290, Carbohydrates: 38g, Saturated Fat: 1g, Protein: 8g, Fat: 10g, Sodium: 420mg, Potassium: 480mg, Fiber: 6g, Sugar: 6g, Vitamin C: 24mg, Calcium: 65mg, Iron: 2.8mg

Ingredients:
- 1 cup [160g] cooked and mashed sweet corn kernels
- 1/2 cup [80g] chopped red bell pepper
- 1/2 cup [75g] chopped zucchini
- 1/4 cup [40g] cooked quinoa
- 2 tbsp chopped fresh cilantro
- 2 tbsp whole-wheat flour
- 1 tbsp olive oil
- 2 cloves minced garlic
- 1/2 tsp smoked paprika
- 1/4 tsp black pepper
- 1/4 tsp sea salt

Directions:
1. Preheat the air fryer to 375°F [190°C].
2. In a large bowl, combine the mashed sweet corn, chopped bell pepper, zucchini, cooked quinoa, minced garlic, smoked paprika, black pepper, and sea salt. Mix well until evenly combined.
3. Add the flour and chopped cilantro to the mixture. Stir thoroughly until a slightly sticky dough forms.
4. Divide the mixture into 4 equal portions and shape each into a small patty about 1/2 inch [1.25 cm] thick.
5. Lightly brush the air fryer basket with olive oil and arrange the patties in a single layer, ensuring they do not touch.
6. Air fry for 10 minutes, then carefully flip the patties and continue air frying for an additional 10 minutes, or until golden and crispy.
7. Remove the cakes from the air fryer and let them cool slightly before serving.

Air-Fried Tempeh Veggie Skewers

- Time: 30 minutes
- Serving Size: 2 servings
- Prep Time: 15 minutes
- Cook Time: 15 minutes

Each Serving Has:
Calories: 280, Carbohydrates: 22g, Saturated Fat: 2g, Protein: 19g, Fat: 15g, Sodium: 430mg, Potassium: 620mg, Fiber: 6g, Sugar: 7g, Vitamin C: 48mg, Calcium: 120mg, Iron: 3.5mg

Ingredients:
- 1 cup [150g] cubed tempeh, steamed
- 1/2 cup [75g] diced red bell pepper
- 1/2 cup [75g] diced zucchini
- 1/2 cup [80g] diced red onion
- 1 tbsp olive oil
- 2 tbsp low-sodium soy sauce
- 1 tbsp lime juice
- 2 tsp maple syrup
- 1 tsp smoked paprika
- 1/2 tsp garlic powder
- 1/4 tsp black pepper

Directions:
1. Preheat the air fryer to 375°F [190°C].
2. In a large bowl, combine the cubed tempeh, diced bell pepper, zucchini, and onion.
3. In a small bowl, whisk together olive oil, soy sauce, lime juice, maple syrup, smoked paprika, garlic powder, and black pepper to create a flavorful marinade.
4. Pour the marinade over the tempeh and vegetables, tossing gently to ensure everything is evenly coated. Let it sit for 5 minutes to allow the flavors to absorb.
5. Thread the marinated tempeh and vegetables alternately onto skewers.
6. Place the skewers in the air fryer basket in a single layer.
7. Air-fry for 15 minutes, turning the skewers halfway through cooking to ensure even browning.
8. Remove the skewers from the air fryer and serve.

Roasted Root Veggie Samosas

- Time: 40 minutes
- Serving Size: 2 servings
- Prep Time: 20 minutes
- Cook Time: 20 minutes

Each Serving Has:
Calories: 310, Carbohydrates: 45g, Saturated Fat: 1.5g, Protein: 9g, Fat: 10g, Sodium: 450mg, Potassium: 720mg, Fiber: 8g, Sugar: 7g, Vitamin C: 32mg, Calcium: 90mg, Iron: 3.8mg

Ingredients:
- 1/2 cup [75g] diced sweet potato, peeled
- 1/2 cup [75g] diced carrot, peeled
- 1/2 cup [75g] diced parsnip, peeled
- 1/2 cup [90g] cooked green peas
- 1/2 cup [60g] chopped red onion
- 2 tbsp chopped fresh cilantro
- 1 tbsp olive oil
- 1 tsp curry powder
- 1/2 tsp ground cumin
- 1/2 tsp smoked paprika
- 1/4 tsp ground turmeric
- 1/4 tsp black pepper
- 1/2 tsp sea salt
- 2 whole-grain pita breads

Directions:
1. Preheat the air fryer to 375°F [190°C].
2. In a mixing bowl, combine the diced sweet potato, carrot, parsnip, and chopped onion.
3. Drizzle the olive oil over the vegetables and toss them with curry powder, cumin, smoked paprika, turmeric, black pepper, and sea salt until evenly coated.
4. Arrange the seasoned vegetables in a single layer in the air fryer basket. Cook for 15 minutes, shaking the basket halfway through to ensure even roasting.
5. Remove the roasted vegetables and transfer them back to the mixing bowl. Stir in the cooked green peas and chopped cilantro.
6. Slice the whole-grain pita breads in half to create pockets. Gently stuff each pocket with the veggie mixture, pressing slightly to pack the filling.
7. Place the stuffed pita pockets back into the air fryer basket. Air fry for an additional 5 minutes to crisp the pita.
8. Remove the samosas from the air fryer and serve.

CHAPTER 4: LUNCHES ◊ 57

Mushroom Brown Rice Nori Wraps

Time: 35 minutes
Serving Size: 2 servings
Prep Time: 20 minutes
Cook Time: 15 minutes

Each Serving Has:
Calories: 285, Carbohydrates: 38g, Saturated Fat: 0.8g, Protein: 9g, Fat: 7g, Sodium: 460mg, Potassium: 720mg, Fiber: 5g, Sugar: 3g, Vitamin C: 22mg, Calcium: 60mg, Iron: 3.1mg

Ingredients:
- 1 cup [150g] cooked brown rice, cooled
- 1 cup [100g] chopped button mushrooms
- 1/2 cup [60g] chopped red bell pepper
- 1/4 cup [30g] chopped scallions
- 1 tbsp low-sodium tamari
- 1 tbsp olive oil
- 1/2 tsp black pepper
- 1/2 tsp smoked paprika
- 4 sheets nori seaweed

Directions:
1. Preheat the air fryer to 375°F [190°C].
2. In a non-stick pan over medium heat, sauté the chopped mushrooms, bell peppers, and scallions in olive oil for 5 minutes, until softened.
3. Stir in the cooked brown rice, tamari, black pepper, and smoked paprika. Cook for an additional 2 minutes, stirring thoroughly until the flavors have combined. Remove from heat and let cool slightly.
4. Lay out one sheet of nori with the rough side facing up. Place 1/4 of the rice mixture along one edge of the nori and roll tightly into a log. Repeat with the remaining nori sheets.
5. Lightly spray the nori wraps with water to help them seal.
6. Arrange the wraps in a single layer in the air fryer basket. Cook for 10–12 minutes, turning once halfway through, until the nori becomes crispy and golden brown on both sides.
7. Let the wraps cool for 2–3 minutes before slicing into bite-sized pieces.

Chapter 5: Dinners

Cauliflower-Lentil Kofta

⏲ Time: 45 minutes		🍽 Serving Size: 2 servings	
🥗 Prep Time: 20 minutes		👨‍🍳 Cook Time: 25 minutes	

Each Serving Has:
Calories: 268, Carbohydrates: 32g, Saturated Fat: 0.8g, Protein: 14g, Fat: 6g, Sodium: 412mg, Potassium: 785mg, Fiber: 12g, Sugar: 6g, Vitamin C: 68mg, Calcium: 102mg, Iron: 5.1mg

Ingredients:
- 2 cups [200g] chopped cauliflower florets
- 1/2 cup [100g] cooked green lentils, drained
- 1/4 cup [30g] chopped red onion
- 1/4 cup [30g] grated carrot
- 2 tbsp chickpea flour
- 2 tbsp chopped fresh cilantro
- 1 tbsp lemon juice
- 1 tbsp olive oil (+ 1/2 tsp extra for brushing)
- 2 tsp ground cumin
- 1 tsp ground coriander
- 1/2 tsp smoked paprika
- 1/2 tsp garlic powder
- 1/4 tsp ground turmeric
- 1/2 tsp sea salt

Directions:
1. Preheat the air fryer to 375°F [190°C].
2. In a mixing bowl, combine the chopped cauliflower florets, cooked lentils, chopped onion, and grated carrot. Mix thoroughly to distribute the vegetables and lentils evenly.
3. Add the chickpea flour, chopped cilantro, lemon juice, olive oil, cumin, coriander, smoked paprika, garlic powder, turmeric, and sea salt to the bowl. Mix until a thick, cohesive mixture forms.
4. Using clean hands, shape the mixture into 8 small oblong kofta shapes, pressing firmly to ensure they hold together.
5. Brush the air fryer basket with a small amount of olive oil to prevent sticking.
6. Arrange the koftas in a single layer in the air fryer basket, ensuring there is space between each for optimal air circulation.
7. Air fry for 25 minutes, flipping the koftas halfway through cooking to achieve an even, golden-brown exterior.
8. Remove the koftas from the air fryer and serve hot.

Air-Fried Tofu Steak with Chimichurri

- Time: 35 minutes
- Serving Size: 2 servings
- Prep Time: 15 minutes
- Cook Time: 20 minutes

Each Serving Has:
Calories: 320, Carbohydrates: 12g, Saturated Fat: 1g, Protein: 22g, Fat: 22g, Sodium: 410mg, Potassium: 650mg, Fiber: 3g, Sugar: 2g, Vitamin C: 18mg, Calcium: 450mg, Iron: 4.2mg

Ingredients:
- 1 block [400g] extra-firm tofu, pressed and sliced into 4 steaks
- 1 tbsp olive oil
- 1 tbsp low-sodium tamari
- 1/2 tsp smoked paprika
- 1/4 tsp black pepper
- 1 cup [30g] chopped fresh parsley
- 1/2 cup [15g] chopped fresh cilantro
- 2 tbsp lime juice
- 1 tbsp olive oil
- 1 tbsp red wine vinegar
- 2 cloves minced garlic
- 1/4 tsp red chili flakes
- 1/4 tsp sea salt

Directions:
1. Preheat the air fryer to 375°F [190°C].
2. In a small bowl, whisk together the olive oil, tamari, smoked paprika, and black pepper.
3. Brush the tofu steaks evenly with the marinade mixture on all sides.
4. Arrange the tofu steaks in a single layer in the air fryer basket.
5. Cook for 20 minutes, flipping the steaks halfway through for even browning.
6. While the tofu cooks, prepare the chimichurri sauce by combining the chopped parsley, cilantro, lime juice, olive oil, red wine vinegar, minced garlic, red chili flakes, and sea salt in a bowl. Mix well and set aside.
7. Once the tofu steaks are crisp and golden, remove from the air fryer and let rest for 2 minutes.
8. Serve hot, topped with chimichurri sauce.

Spaghetti Squash Veggie Balls

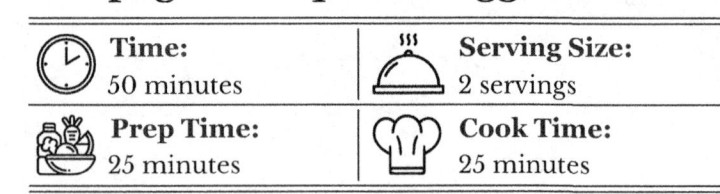

- Time: 50 minutes
- Serving Size: 2 servings
- Prep Time: 25 minutes
- Cook Time: 25 minutes

Each Serving Has:
Calories: 242, Carbohydrates: 29g, Saturated Fat: 0.7g, Protein: 9g, Fat: 5g, Sodium: 390mg, Potassium: 845mg, Fiber: 10g, Sugar: 8g, Vitamin C: 52mg, Calcium: 95mg, Iron: 4.7mg

Ingredients:
- 2 cups [200g] cooked and shredded spaghetti squash
- 1/2 cup [90g] cooked chickpeas, mashed
- 1/4 cup [30g] chopped red bell pepper
- 1/4 cup [30g] chopped yellow onion
- 2 tbsp rolled oats, ground into flour
- 2 tbsp chopped fresh parsley
- 1 tbsp lemon juice
- 1 tbsp olive oil (+ 1/2 tsp extra for brushing)
- 2 tsp ground cumin
- 1/2 tsp smoked paprika
- 1/2 tsp garlic powder
- 1/4 tsp sea salt

Directions:
1. Preheat the air fryer to 375°F [190°C].
2. In a mixing bowl, combine the cooked squash, mashed chickpeas, chopped bell pepper, and onion. Mix well to ensure the ingredients are distributed evenly.
3. Add the oat flour, chopped parsley, lemon juice, olive oil, cumin, smoked paprika, garlic powder, and sea salt to the bowl. Stir thoroughly until a firm mixture forms.
4. Using your hands, shape the mixture into 8 equal-sized balls, pressing gently to hold their shape.
5. Brush the air fryer basket with a small amount of olive oil to prevent sticking.
6. Arrange the veggie balls in a single layer in the air fryer basket, leaving space between each for proper air circulation.
7. Air fry for 25 minutes, shaking the basket or gently turning the veggie balls halfway through to ensure even browning.
8. Remove the balls from the air fryer and serve.

Butternut Chickpea Hash Stack

⏲ Time: 35 minutes	🍽 Serving Size: 2 servings
🥗 Prep Time: 15 minutes	👨‍🍳 Cook Time: 20 minutes

Each Serving Has:
Calories: 310, Carbohydrates: 42g, Saturated Fat: 1g, Protein: 10g, Fat: 12g, Sodium: 420mg, Potassium: 760mg, Fiber: 9g, Sugar: 8g, Vitamin C: 34mg, Calcium: 120mg, Iron: 3.8mg

Ingredients:
- 2 cups [300g] small diced butternut squash
- 1 cup [165g] cooked and mashed chickpeas
- 1/2 cup [80g] chopped red bell pepper
- 1/4 cup [30g] chopped red onion
- 1 tbsp olive oil
- 1 tsp smoked paprika
- 1/2 tsp ground cumin
- 1/2 tsp garlic powder
- 1/4 tsp black pepper
- 1/4 tsp sea salt
- 2 tbsp chopped fresh cilantro

Directions:
1. Preheat the air fryer to 375°F [190°C].
2. In a mixing bowl, combine the diced squash, olive oil, smoked paprika, cumin, garlic powder, black pepper, and sea salt. Toss until evenly coated.
3. Arrange the seasoned butternut squash in a single layer in the air fryer basket. Cook for 15 minutes, shaking the basket halfway through for even roasting.
4. While the squash is roasting, combine the mashed chickpeas, chopped bell pepper, onion, and cilantro in a separate bowl. Mix well to form a chunky hash mixture.
5. Once the butternut squash is cooked and slightly crispy, fold it into the chickpea hash mixture.
6. Using your hands or a ring mold, form the mixture into firm, stackable patties.
7. Place the patties back into the air fryer and cook for an additional 5 minutes to heat through and slightly crisp the edges.
8. Remove the hash stack from the air fryer and serve.

Eggplant-Millet Air Parm

⏲ Time: 45 minutes	🍽 Serving Size: 2 servings
🥗 Prep Time: 20 minutes	👨‍🍳 Cook Time: 25 minutes

Each Serving Has:
Calories: 320, Carbohydrates: 42g, Saturated Fat: 1g, Protein: 10g, Fat: 11g, Sodium: 380mg, Potassium: 790mg, Fiber: 9g, Sugar: 7g, Vitamin C: 22mg, Calcium: 140mg, Iron: 4.1mg

Ingredients:
- 2 cups [300g] sliced eggplant rounds, 1/2-inch thick
- 1 cup [180g] cooked and fluffed millet
- 1/2 cup [120ml] low-sodium tomato sauce
- 1/2 cup [80g] chopped red bell pepper
- 1/4 cup [30g] chopped red onion
- 1 tbsp olive oil
- 1 tsp dried oregano
- 1/4 tsp black pepper
- 1/4 tsp sea salt
- 2 tbsp chopped fresh basil

Directions:
1. Preheat the air fryer to 375°F [190°C].
2. In a mixing bowl, toss the eggplant rounds with olive oil, black pepper, and sea salt until evenly coated.
3. Arrange the seasoned eggplant slices in a single layer in the air fryer basket. Cook for 12 minutes, flipping them halfway through for even browning.
4. While the eggplant cooks, combine the cooked millet, chopped bell pepper, onion, oregano, nutritional yeast, and half of the basil in a separate bowl. Mix thoroughly to create a flavorful millet stuffing.
5. Remove the eggplant rounds from the air fryer and top each slice with a spoonful of the millet mixture, gently pressing it down to form a compact layer.
6. Spoon a small amount of tomato sauce over each millet-topped eggplant round.
7. Return the assembled eggplant stacks to the air fryer and cook for an additional 8 minutes to heat through and slightly crisp the tops.
8. Garnish with the remaining basil before serving.

CHAPTER 5: DINNERS

Moroccan-Spiced Carrot Patties

⏰ Time: 40 minutes	🍽 Serving Size: 2 servings
🥗 Prep Time: 20 minutes	👨‍🍳 Cook Time: 20 minutes

Each Serving Has:
Calories: 290, Carbohydrates: 38g, Saturated Fat: 1g, Protein: 9g, Fat: 10g, Sodium: 410mg, Potassium: 870mg, Fiber: 8g, Sugar: 10g, Vitamin C: 20mg, Calcium: 120mg, Iron: 4mg

Ingredients:
- 1 1/2 cups [180g] grated carrots
- 1/2 cup [90g] cooked chickpeas, mashed
- 1/4 cup [40g] chopped red onion
- 1/4 cup [30g] chopped fresh parsley
- 2 tbsp chickpea flour
- 1 tbsp olive oil
- 1 tbsp lemon juice
- 1 tsp ground cumin
- 1/2 tsp ground coriander
- 1/2 tsp smoked paprika
- 1/4 tsp ground cinnamon
- 1/4 tsp sea salt
- 1/4 tsp black pepper

Directions:
1. Preheat the air fryer to 375°F [190°C].
2. In a mixing bowl, combine the grated carrots, mashed chickpeas, chopped onion, parsley, chickpea flour, lemon juice, olive oil, cumin, coriander, smoked paprika, cinnamon, sea salt, and black pepper. Mix thoroughly until a cohesive mixture forms.
3. Shape the mixture into 4 equal-sized patties, pressing firmly to maintain shape.
4. Arrange the patties in a single layer in the air fryer basket.
5. Cook for 20 minutes, flipping the patties halfway through to ensure even crisping.
6. Remove the patties from the air fryer and serve hot.

Sweet Potato & Kale Air Casserole

⏰ Time: 45 minutes	🍽 Serving Size: 2 servings
🥗 Prep Time: 15 minutes	👨‍🍳 Cook Time: 30 minutes

Each Serving Has:
Calories: 320, Carbohydrates: 45g, Saturated Fat: 1g, Protein: 10g, Fat: 12g, Sodium: 410mg, Potassium: 980mg, Fiber: 9g, Sugar: 12g, Vitamin C: 45mg, Calcium: 180mg, Iron: 4.2mg

Ingredients:
- 2 cups [280g] peeled and diced sweet potatoes
- 1 1/2 cups [90g] chopped fresh kale, stems removed
- 1/2 cup [120ml] low-sodium vegetable broth
- 1/2 cup [90g] cooked chickpeas, rinsed and drained
- 1/4 cup [30g] chopped red onion
- 2 tbsp nutritional yeast
- 1 tbsp olive oil
- 1 tsp garlic powder
- 1/2 tsp smoked paprika
- 1/2 tsp ground cumin
- 1/4 tsp ground turmeric
- 1/4 tsp sea salt
- 1/4 tsp black pepper

Directions:
1. Preheat the air fryer to 375°F [190°C].
2. In a mixing bowl, combine diced sweet potatoes, chopped kale, onion, cooked chickpeas, vegetable broth, olive oil, nutritional yeast, garlic powder, smoked paprika, cumin, turmeric, sea salt, and black pepper. Toss thoroughly to coat all ingredients evenly.
3. Transfer the mixture into an air fryer-safe casserole dish or a heat-resistant baking dish that fits into the air fryer basket. Spread the mixture evenly.
4. Air fry for 30 minutes, stirring once halfway through to ensure even cooking.
5. Remove from the air fryer and serve hot.

Zucchini Lentil Lasagna Cups

Time: 45 minutes	Serving Size: 2 servings
Prep Time: 20 minutes	Cook Time: 25 minutes

Each Serving Has:
Calories: 265, Carbohydrates: 34g, Saturated Fat: 1g, Protein: 13g, Fat: 9g, Sodium: 340mg, Potassium: 910mg, Fiber: 11g, Sugar: 7g, Vitamin C: 30mg, Calcium: 92mg, Iron: 4.1mg

Ingredients:
- 1 cup [130g] grated zucchini, squeezed dry
- 1/2 cup [100g] cooked green lentils, drained
- 1/2 cup [120ml] salt-free tomato sauce
- 1/4 cup [40g] chopped yellow onion
- 1/4 cup [25g] grated carrot
- 1/4 cup [25g] chopped red bell pepper
- 2 tbsp ground flaxseed
- 2 tbsp oat flour
- 1 tbsp olive oil
- 1/2 tsp dried oregano
- 1/4 tsp crushed red pepper flakes
- 1/4 tsp sea salt
- 1/4 tsp black pepper

Directions:
1. Preheat the air fryer to 375°F [190°C].
2. In a mixing bowl, combine the grated zucchini, cooked lentils, tomato sauce, chopped onion, bell pepper, and grated carrot. Stir until evenly distributed.
3. Add the ground flaxseed, oat flour, olive oil, oregano, red pepper flakes, sea salt, and black pepper. Mix thoroughly until the mixture thickens and holds together.
4. Lightly grease or line six silicone muffin cups that fit in your air fryer basket. Evenly distribute the mixture into the cups and gently press to form compact lasagna cups.
5. Arrange the muffin cups in a single layer in the air fryer basket.
6. Air fry for 25 minutes, checking after 15 minutes and rotating if needed for even cooking.
7. Let the lasagna cups cool for 5 minutes before carefully removing them from the cups and serving.

Crunchy Quinoa-Stuffed Peppers

Time: 40 minutes	Serving Size: 2 servings
Prep Time: 15 minutes	Cook Time: 25 minutes

Each Serving Has:
Calories: 310, Carbohydrates: 42g, Saturated Fat: 1g, Protein: 11g, Fat: 11g, Sodium: 340mg, Potassium: 950mg, Fiber: 9g, Sugar: 7g, Vitamin C: 120mg, Calcium: 60mg, Iron: 4.5mg

Ingredients:
- 2 medium [300g] red bell peppers, tops removed and seeds discarded
- 1 cup [185g] cooked quinoa, cooled
- 1/2 cup [100g] cooked black beans, rinsed and drained
- 1/2 cup [100g] chopped zucchini
- 1/4 cup [40g] chopped red onion
- 1/4 cup [60ml] salt-free tomato sauce
- 2 tbsp chopped fresh cilantro
- 1 tbsp olive oil
- 1 tsp smoked paprika
- 1/2 tsp ground cumin
- 1/4 tsp garlic powder
- 1/4 tsp sea salt
- 1/4 tsp black pepper

Directions:
1. Preheat the air fryer to 375°F [190°C].
2. In a mixing bowl, combine the cooked quinoa, black beans, chopped zucchini, onion, tomato sauce, cilantro, olive oil, smoked paprika, cumin, garlic powder, sea salt, and black pepper. Mix thoroughly until evenly combined.
3. Stuff the hollowed bell peppers tightly with the quinoa mixture, pressing down gently to pack the filling.
4. Place the stuffed peppers upright in the air fryer basket. If they don't stand securely, trim a small flat base at the bottom of each pepper.
5. Air fry for 25 minutes, checking after 15 minutes to ensure even cooking.
6. Once the tops are slightly crisp and the peppers are tender, remove from the air fryer.
7. Let the stuffed peppers cool for 5 minutes before serving.

CHAPTER 5: DINNERS

Broccoli-Cauliflower Curry Bites

Time: 35 minutes
Serving Size: 2 servings
Prep Time: 15 minutes
Cook Time: 20 minutes

Each Serving Has:
Calories: 210, Carbohydrates: 24g, Saturated Fat: 1g, Protein: 9g, Fat: 9g, Sodium: 310mg, Potassium: 820mg, Fiber: 7g, Sugar: 4g, Vitamin C: 95mg, Calcium: 110mg, Iron: 3.8mg

Ingredients:
- 1 cup [100g] chopped broccoli florets
- 1 cup [100g] chopped cauliflower florets
- 1/2 cup [120g] cooked and mashed chickpeas
- 1/4 cup [30g] grated carrot
- 2 tbsp chopped fresh cilantro
- 1/4 cup [30g] chopped red onion
- 1/4 cup [30g] chickpea flour
- 1 tbsp olive oil
- 1 tsp curry powder
- 1/2 tsp ground turmeric
- 1/4 tsp ground cumin
- 1/4 tsp sea salt
- 1/4 tsp black pepper

Directions:
1. Preheat the air fryer to 375°F [190°C].
2. In a large bowl, combine the chopped broccoli, cauliflower, mashed chickpeas, grated carrot, chopped cilantro, onion, chickpea flour, olive oil, curry powder, turmeric, cumin, sea salt, and black pepper. Mix until a cohesive mixture forms.
3. Using your hands, form the mixture into small bite-sized patties, about 1.5 inches [4cm] in diameter.
4. Arrange the patties in a single layer in the air fryer basket, ensuring they don't touch.
5. Air fry for 20 minutes, flipping the bites halfway through cooking to ensure even crisping.
6. Let the bites cool for 5 minutes before serving.

Curried Rice and Chickpea Cakes

Time: 40 minutes
Serving Size: 2 servings
Prep Time: 15 minutes
Cook Time: 25 minutes

Each Serving Has:
Calories: 280, Carbohydrates: 38g, Saturated Fat: 1g, Protein: 11g, Fat: 9g, Sodium: 310mg, Potassium: 640mg, Fiber: 8g, Sugar: 4g, Vitamin C: 10mg, Calcium: 90mg, Iron: 3.6mg

Ingredients:
- 1 cup [200g] cooked brown rice, cooled
- 1/2 cup [120g] mashed cooked chickpeas
- 1/4 cup [30g] chopped red bell pepper
- 1/4 cup [30g] chopped red onion
- 2 tbsp chopped fresh cilantro
- 1/4 cup [30g] chickpea flour
- 1 tbsp olive oil
- 1 tsp curry powder
- 1/2 tsp ground turmeric
- 1/4 tsp ground cumin
- 1/4 tsp garlic powder
- 1/4 tsp sea salt
- 1/4 tsp black pepper

Directions:
1. Preheat the air fryer to 375°F [190°C].
2. In a large bowl, combine the cooked brown rice, mashed chickpeas, chopped bell pepper, onion, cilantro, chickpea flour, olive oil, curry powder, turmeric, cumin, garlic powder, sea salt, and black pepper. Mix until the ingredients hold together firmly.
3. Shape the mixture into 4 equal patties, pressing them gently to keep their form.
4. Arrange the patties in a single layer in the air fryer basket, ensuring space between them.
5. Air fry for 25 minutes, flipping the patties halfway through for even crisping.
6. Allow the patties to cool for 5 minutes before serving.

Tofu-Pumpkin Rice Bake

Time: 50 minutes	Serving Size: 2 servings
Prep Time: 15 minutes	Cook Time: 35 minutes

Each Serving Has:
Calories: 325, Carbohydrates: 38g, Saturated Fat: 1g, Protein: 17g, Fat: 10g, Sodium: 410mg, Potassium: 710mg, Fiber: 6g, Sugar: 5g, Vitamin C: 16mg, Calcium: 320mg, Iron: 4.2mg

Ingredients:
- 1 cup [200g] cooked brown rice, cooled
- 1/2 cup [120g] mashed cooked pumpkin
- 1/2 cup [120g] crumbled firm tofu, pressed
- 1/4 cup [30g] chopped red bell pepper
- 1/4 cup [30g] chopped red onion
- 1 tbsp olive oil
- 2 tbsp nutritional yeast
- 1 tsp smoked paprika
- 1/2 tsp ground cumin
- 1/2 tsp ground turmeric
- 1/4 tsp black pepper
- 1/2 tsp sea salt
- 1 tbsp chopped fresh parsley

Directions:
1. Preheat the air fryer to 375°F [190°C].
2. In a mixing bowl, combine the cooked brown rice, mashed pumpkin, crumbled tofu, chopped bell pepper, onion, olive oil, nutritional yeast, smoked paprika, cumin, turmeric, black pepper, sea salt, and chopped parsley. Mix until well incorporated and slightly sticky.
3. Transfer the mixture into two small air fryer-safe ramekins or silicone muffin molds, pressing the mixture down firmly to create a compact bake.
4. Place the ramekins or molds into the air fryer basket.
5. Air fry for 35 minutes until the tops are golden and slightly crisp.
6. Let the rice bake cool for 5 minutes before removing from the molds and serving.

Mushroom-Stuffed Polenta Squares

Time: 50 minutes	Serving Size: 2 servings
Prep Time: 20 minutes	Cook Time: 30 minutes

Each Serving Has:
Calories: 310, Carbohydrates: 38g, Saturated Fat: 1g, Protein: 9g, Fat: 12g, Sodium: 340mg, Potassium: 720mg, Fiber: 5g, Sugar: 4g, Vitamin C: 14mg, Calcium: 60mg, Iron: 3.8mg

Ingredients:
- 1 cup [240ml] low-sodium vegetable broth
- 1/2 cup [80g] dry polenta (cornmeal)
- 1/2 cup [100g] chopped cremini mushrooms
- 1/4 cup [30g] chopped red onion
- 1/4 cup [30g] chopped red bell pepper
- 1 tbsp olive oil
- 1/2 tsp garlic powder
- 1/2 tsp sea salt

Directions:
1. Preheat the air fryer to 375°F [190°C].
2. In a saucepan, boil the vegetable broth, then whisk in the polenta. Cook on low, stirring often, until thickened, 5–7 minutes. Remove from heat and let cool.
3. In a skillet, heat olive oil over medium heat. Sauté the chopped mushrooms, onion, and bell pepper for 5-6 minutes, until softened. Stir in the garlic powder and sea salt. Remove from the heat.
4. Line a small square pan with parchment paper. Spread half the polenta evenly, layer with the mushroom mixture, then top with remaining polenta, pressing gently to form a solid layer.
5. Chill in the refrigerator for 15 minutes to allow the layers to firm up.
6. Once set, cut the polenta into 4 squares and transfer them to the air fryer basket.
7. Air fry for 15 minutes, flipping halfway through, until the edges are crisp and golden.
8. Let cool for 5 minutes before serving.

Roasted Brussels Veggie Mix

- **Time:** 30 minutes
- **Serving Size:** 2 servings
- **Prep Time:** 10 minutes
- **Cook Time:** 20 minutes

Each Serving Has:
Calories: 180, Carbohydrates: 22g, Saturated Fat: 1g, Protein: 5g, Fat: 9g, Sodium: 320mg, Potassium: 620mg, Fiber: 7g, Sugar: 7g, Vitamin C: 85mg, Calcium: 60mg, Iron: 2.5mg

Ingredients:
- 2 cups [200g] halved Brussels sprouts
- 1/2 cup [75g] diced red bell pepper
- 1/2 cup [75g] diced zucchini
- 1/2 cup [75g] thinly sliced red onion
- 1 tbsp olive oil
- 1/2 tsp garlic powder
- 1/2 tsp smoked paprika
- 1/4 tsp black pepper
- 1/2 tsp sea salt
- 1 tbsp chopped fresh parsley

Directions:
1. Preheat the air fryer to 375°F [190°C].
2. In a mixing bowl, combine the halved Brussels sprouts, diced bell pepper, zucchini, and sliced onion.
3. Drizzle the vegetables with the olive oil and toss them with the garlic powder, smoked paprika, black pepper, and sea salt until evenly coated.
4. Arrange the vegetable mixture in a single layer in the air fryer basket.
5. Cook for 20 minutes, shaking the basket halfway through to ensure even roasting.
6. Garnish with the chopped parsley before serving.

Cabbage-Wrapped Spiced Lentils

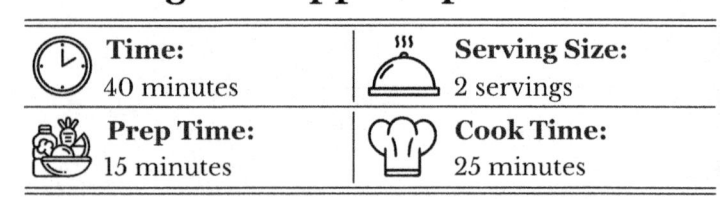

- **Time:** 40 minutes
- **Serving Size:** 2 servings
- **Prep Time:** 15 minutes
- **Cook Time:** 25 minutes

Each Serving Has:
Calories: 230, Carbohydrates: 33g, Saturated Fat: 1g, Protein: 12g, Fat: 6g, Sodium: 340mg, Potassium: 710mg, Fiber: 11g, Sugar: 6g, Vitamin C: 78mg, Calcium: 95mg, Iron: 4.2mg

Ingredients:
- 6 large [180g] steamed green cabbage leaves
- 1 cup [200g] cooked brown lentils
- 1/2 cup [100g] chopped red bell pepper
- 1/4 cup [40g] chopped red onion
- 1/2 cup [90g] grated carrot
- 1 tbsp olive oil
- 1/2 tsp ground cumin
- 1/2 tsp smoked paprika
- 1/4 tsp ground turmeric
- 1/2 tsp sea salt
- 1/4 tsp black pepper
- 1 tbsp chopped fresh cilantro

Directions:
1. Preheat the air fryer to 375°F [190°C].
2. In a mixing bowl, combine the cooked lentils, chopped bell pepper, onion, and grated carrot.
3. Add the olive oil, cumin, smoked paprika, turmeric, sea salt, and black pepper. Mix thoroughly until the filling is well combined and evenly spiced.
4. Place a steamed cabbage leaf on a flat surface, spoon a generous portion of the lentil mixture into the center, and roll tightly to form a secure wrap. Repeat with the remaining leaves and filling.
5. Arrange the cabbage wraps in a single layer in the air fryer basket.
6. Cook for 25 minutes, turning the wraps halfway through to ensure even cooking and crisp edges.
7. Garnish with the chopped cilantro before serving.

Air-Fried Gnocchi with Herbs

Time: 25 minutes
Serving Size: 2 servings
Prep Time: 10 minutes
Cook Time: 15 minutes

Each Serving Has:
Calories: 320, Carbohydrates: 48g, Saturated Fat: 1g, Protein: 10g, Fat: 9g, Sodium: 420mg, Potassium: 610mg, Fiber: 7g, Sugar: 3g, Vitamin C: 22mg, Calcium: 75mg, Iron: 3.5mg

Ingredients:
- 2 cups [300g] cooked and cooled whole-wheat potato gnocchi
- 1 tbsp olive oil
- 1/2 cup [100g] chopped red bell pepper
- 1/2 cup [75g] chopped zucchini
- 1/4 cup [40g] thinly sliced red onion
- 1 tbsp chopped fresh basil
- 1 tbsp chopped fresh parsley
- 1/2 tsp dried oregano
- 1/2 tsp garlic powder
- 1/4 tsp black pepper
- 1/2 tsp sea salt

Directions:
1. Preheat the air fryer to 375°F [190°C].
2. In a mixing bowl, toss the cooked gnocchi with olive oil, chopped bell pepper, zucchini, and sliced onion.
3. Sprinkle the mixture with the garlic powder, oregano, sea salt, and black pepper. Toss again until the gnocchi and vegetables are evenly coated with seasoning.
4. Arrange the gnocchi mixture in a single layer in the air fryer basket.
5. Cook for 15 minutes, shaking the basket halfway through for even crisping.
6. Remove from the air fryer and immediately toss with the chopped basil and parsley for a burst of fresh flavor. Serve hot.

Crispy Eggplant and Corn Patties

Time: 35 minutes
Serving Size: 2 servings
Prep Time: 15 minutes
Cook Time: 20 minutes

Each Serving Has:
Calories: 280, Carbohydrates: 38g, Saturated Fat: 1g, Protein: 8g, Fat: 10g, Sodium: 360mg, Potassium: 680mg, Fiber: 9g, Sugar: 7g, Vitamin C: 24mg, Calcium: 65mg, Iron: 2.8mg

Ingredients:
- 1 1/2 cups [225g] grated eggplant
- 1 cup [160g] cooked corn kernels
- 1/2 cup [75g] chopped red bell pepper
- 1/4 cup [40g] chopped green onions
- 1/2 cup [80g] cooked quinoa
- 1 tbsp ground flaxseeds
- 3 tbsp water
- 1 tbsp olive oil
- 1 tsp smoked paprika
- 1/2 tsp garlic powder
- 1/2 tsp ground cumin
- 1/4 tsp black pepper
- 1/2 tsp sea salt

Directions:
1. Preheat the air fryer to 375°F [190°C].
2. In a small bowl, combine the ground flaxseeds and water to create a flax "egg." Let it sit for 5 minutes to thicken.
3. In a mixing bowl, combine the grated eggplant, cooked corn kernels, chopped bell pepper, green onions, and cooked quinoa.
4. Add the flax "egg," olive oil, smoked paprika, garlic powder, cumin, sea salt, and black pepper. Mix thoroughly until the mixture forms a cohesive texture.
5. Shape the mixture into 4 equal patties, pressing firmly to form compact shapes.
6. Arrange the patties in a single layer in the air fryer basket.
7. Cook for 20 minutes, flipping the patties carefully at the 10-minute mark for even crisping.
8. Remove the patties from the air fryer and serve.

Chickpea Mushroom Stroganoff Bites

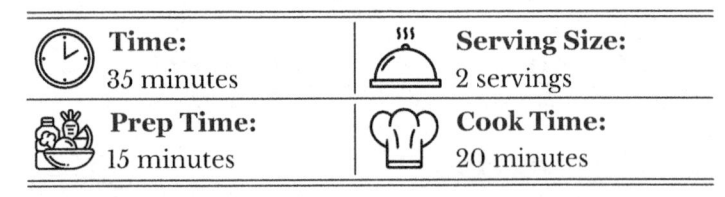

⏱ Time: 35 minutes	🍽 Serving Size: 2 servings
🥗 Prep Time: 15 minutes	👨‍🍳 Cook Time: 20 minutes

Each Serving Has:
Calories: 310, Carbohydrates: 36g, Saturated Fat: 1g, Protein: 14g, Fat: 11g, Sodium: 390mg, Potassium: 720mg, Fiber: 10g, Sugar: 5g, Vitamin C: 22mg, Calcium: 85mg, Iron: 3.4mg

Ingredients:
- 1 cup [160g] cooked and mashed chickpeas
- 1 cup [150g] chopped cremini mushrooms
- 1/2 cup [80g] chopped yellow onion
- 1/2 cup [80g] cooked quinoa
- 1 tbsp ground flaxseeds
- 3 tbsp water
- 2 tbsp nutritional yeast
- 1 tbsp olive oil
- 1 tsp smoked paprika
- 1 tsp dried thyme
- 1/2 tsp garlic powder
- 1/4 tsp sea salt

Directions:
1. Preheat the air fryer to 375°F [190°C].
2. In a small bowl, combine the ground flaxseeds and water to form a flax "egg." Let it sit for 5 minutes to thicken.
3. In a skillet over medium heat, sauté the chopped mushrooms and onion in olive oil for 5-7 minutes, until softened. Let them cool.
4. In a bowl, combine the chickpeas, quinoa, mushrooms, nutritional yeast, smoked paprika, thyme, garlic powder, and sea salt.
5. Stir in the flax "egg" and mix until a firm, moldable mixture forms, then form 6 small bites, pressing gently to hold shape.
6. Arrange the bites in a single layer in the air fryer basket.
7. Cook for 20 minutes, flipping carefully at the 10-minute mark for even browning.
8. Remove the bites from the air fryer and serve.

Carrot-Zucchini Noodle Balls

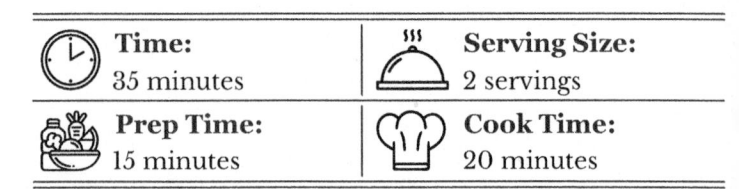

⏱ Time: 35 minutes	🍽 Serving Size: 2 servings
🥗 Prep Time: 15 minutes	👨‍🍳 Cook Time: 20 minutes

Each Serving Has:
Calories: 265, Carbohydrates: 30g, Saturated Fat: 1g, Protein: 11g, Fat: 10g, Sodium: 380mg, Potassium: 710mg, Fiber: 9g, Sugar: 6g, Vitamin C: 28mg, Calcium: 90mg, Iron: 3.2mg

Ingredients:
- 1 cup [120g] spiralized zucchini noodles, chopped
- 1/2 cup [60g] grated carrot
- 1 cup [160g] cooked and mashed chickpeas
- 1/2 cup [80g] chopped red bell pepper
- 2 tbsp ground flaxseeds
- 5 tbsp water
- 2 tbsp nutritional yeast
- 1 tbsp olive oil (+ 1/2 tsp extra for brushing)
- 1 tsp dried oregano
- 1/2 tsp garlic powder
- 1/4 tsp sea salt

Directions:
1. Preheat the air fryer to 375°F [190°C].
2. In a small bowl, combine the ground flaxseeds and water to form a flax "egg." Let it sit for 5 minutes to thicken.
3. In a bowl, combine the chopped zucchini noodles, bell pepper, grated carrot, mashed chickpeas, nutritional yeast, oregano, garlic powder, and sea salt.
4. Stir in the flax "egg" and mix until cohesive, then shape into 8 small balls, pressing gently to hold shape.
5. Brush the air fryer basket with olive oil and arrange the balls in a single layer.
6. Cook for 20 minutes, flipping carefully at the 10-minute mark for even browning.
7. Remove the balls from the air fryer and serve.

Crunchy Black Bean Tofu Steaks

Time: 35 minutes	Serving Size: 2 servings
Prep Time: 15 minutes	Cook Time: 20 minutes

Each Serving Has:
Calories: 310, Carbohydrates: 24g, Saturated Fat: 1.2g, Protein: 20g, Fat: 14g, Sodium: 420mg, Potassium: 780mg, Fiber: 10g, Sugar: 4g, Vitamin C: 22mg, Calcium: 380mg, Iron: 4.6mg

Ingredients:
- 1 block [400g] extra-firm tofu, pressed and sliced into 4 steaks
- 1 cup [170g] cooked and mashed black beans
- 1/2 cup [60g] grated zucchini
- 1/2 cup [50g] chopped red bell pepper
- 1/4 cup [30g] chopped green onions
- 2 tbsp ground flaxseeds
- 5 tbsp water
- 2 tbsp nutritional yeast
- 1 tbsp olive oil (+ 1/2 tsp extra for brushing)
- 1 tsp smoked paprika
- 1 tsp ground cumin
- 1/2 tsp sea salt

Directions:
1. Preheat the air fryer to 375°F [190°C].
2. In a small bowl, mix the ground flaxseeds and water to form a flax "egg." Let it sit for 5 minutes to thicken.
3. In a bowl, combine the mashed black beans, grated zucchini, chopped bell pepper, and green onions.
4. Stir in the nutritional yeast, smoked paprika, cumin, sea salt, and the prepared flax "egg." Mix until a sticky dough forms.
5. Press the black bean mixture onto one side of each tofu steak in a thick, even layer.
6. Brush the air fryer basket with olive oil and place the tofu steaks coated side up.
7. Cook for 20 minutes, flipping after 10 minutes for even crisping.
8. Remove the steaks from the air fryer and serve.

Creamy Spinach Quinoa Cups

Time: 40 minutes	Serving Size: 2 servings
Prep Time: 15 minutes	Cook Time: 25 minutes

Each Serving Has:
Calories: 285, Carbohydrates: 28g, Saturated Fat: 1.4g, Protein: 13g, Fat: 12g, Sodium: 410mg, Potassium: 740mg, Fiber: 7g, Sugar: 3g, Vitamin C: 24mg, Calcium: 150mg, Iron: 4.2mg

Ingredients:
- 1 cup [185g] cooked quinoa
- 1 cup [30g] chopped fresh spinach
- 1/2 cup [80g] mashed cooked chickpeas
- 1/4 cup [60ml] unsweetened plain plant-based yogurt
- 1/4 cup [30g] chopped red bell pepper
- 2 tbsp nutritional yeast
- 1 tbsp olive oil (+ 1/2 tsp extra for brushing)
- 1 tbsp ground flaxseeds
- 3 tbsp water
- 1 tsp garlic powder
- 1/2 tsp dried oregano
- 1/4 tsp sea salt

Directions:
1. Preheat the air fryer to 375°F [190°C].
2. In a small bowl, combine the ground flaxseeds and water to create a flax "egg." Let it rest for 5 minutes until thickened.
3. In a bowl, mix the cooked quinoa, mashed chickpeas, chopped bell pepper, spinach, and yogurt.
4. Add the nutritional yeast, garlic powder, oregano, sea salt, and the flax "egg." Mix until a uniform batter forms.
5. Grease silicone muffin cups with olive oil, then evenly divide the mixture, pressing firmly to shape compact cups.
6. Place the filled cups into the air fryer basket.
7. Air fry for 25 minutes, checking at 15 minutes to ensure even cooking. The tops should be golden and slightly crisp.
8. Cool for 5 minutes, then carefully remove from the cups and serve.

Air-Fried Vegetable Tikka Parcels

⏲ Time: 45 minutes	🍽 Serving Size: 2 servings
🥗 Prep Time: 20 minutes	👨‍🍳 Cook Time: 25 minutes

Each Serving Has:
Calories: 310, Carbohydrates: 34g, Saturated Fat: 1.2g, Protein: 10g, Fat: 12g, Sodium: 420mg, Potassium: 780mg, Fiber: 8g, Sugar: 6g, Vitamin C: 52mg, Calcium: 140mg, Iron: 3.8mg

Ingredients:
- 1 cup [150g] chopped bell peppers (red, green, yellow)
- 1 cup [200g] steamed and mashed sweet potatoes
- 1/2 cup [90g] cooked green peas
- 1/2 cup [120g] cooked chickpeas, mashed
- 1/4 cup [30g] chopped red onion
- 2 tbsp chickpea flour
- 2 tbsp plain unsweetened plant-based yogurt
- 1 tbsp olive oil
- 1 tbsp lemon juice
- 1 tsp garam masala
- 1/2 tsp ground turmeric
- 1/8 tsp sea salt
- 4 whole-wheat tortilla wraps

Directions:
1. Preheat the air fryer to 375°F [190°C].
2. In a bowl, combine the mashed sweet potatoes, chickpeas, cooked green peas, chopped bell peppers, and onion.
3. Add the chickpea flour, yogurt, lemon juice, garam masala, turmeric, and sea salt. Mix until the mixture forms a cohesive texture.
4. Lay out the whole-wheat tortillas and place equal portions of the filling in the center of each. Fold the edges over to form sealed parcels.
5. Brush the parcels with olive oil and arrange them in a single layer in the air fryer basket.
6. Air fry for 25 minutes, flipping carefully at the 15-minute mark for even crisping.
7. Allow the parcels to cool slightly before serving.

Sweet Corn & Leek Galettes

⏲ Time: 45 minutes	🍽 Serving Size: 2 servings
🥗 Prep Time: 20 minutes	👨‍🍳 Cook Time: 25 minutes

Each Serving Has:
Calories: 285, Carbohydrates: 36g, Saturated Fat: 1.1g, Protein: 9g, Fat: 10g, Sodium: 410mg, Potassium: 720mg, Fiber: 7g, Sugar: 6g, Vitamin C: 45mg, Calcium: 130mg, Iron: 3.4mg

Ingredients:
- 1 cup [150g] fresh or frozen sweet corn kernels, thawed if frozen
- 1 cup [100g] sliced leeks, white and light green parts only
- 1/2 cup [120g] mashed cooked chickpeas
- 1/4 cup [30g] chopped fresh parsley
- 1/4 cup [30g] chickpea flour
- 2 tbsp plain unsweetened plant-based yogurt
- 1 tbsp olive oil
- 1 tbsp lemon juice
- 1 tsp ground coriander
- 1/2 tsp ground turmeric
- 1/2 tsp smoked paprika
- 1/2 tsp sea salt
- 1/4 tsp black pepper

Directions:
1. Preheat the air fryer to 375°F [190°C].
2. In a mixing bowl, combine the mashed chickpeas, sweet corn kernels, sliced leeks, and chopped parsley.
3. Add the chickpea flour, plant-based yogurt, olive oil, lemon juice, coriander, turmeric, smoked paprika, sea salt, and black pepper. Mix thoroughly until the mixture forms a cohesive dough.
4. Divide the mixture into four equal portions and shape each into a small flat disc about 3 inches [7.5 cm] in diameter.
5. Place the galettes in the air fryer basket, ensuring they don't touch each other.
6. Air fry for 25 minutes, flipping the galettes carefully at the 15-minute mark for even browning.
7. Let the galettes cool slightly before serving.

Baked Turmeric Cauliflower Slabs

Time: 40 minutes	Serving Size: 2 servings
Prep Time: 15 minutes	Cook Time: 25 minutes

Each Serving Has:
Calories: 210, Carbohydrates: 18g, Saturated Fat: 1.5g, Protein: 6g, Fat: 14g, Sodium: 380mg, Potassium: 720mg, Fiber: 7g, Sugar: 5g, Vitamin C: 75mg, Calcium: 90mg, Iron: 2.3mg

Ingredients:
- 2 large [500g] cauliflower slabs, cut 1-inch thick from the center of the head
- 2 tbsp olive oil
- 1 tsp ground turmeric
- 1/2 tsp ground cumin
- 1/2 tsp smoked paprika
- 1/4 tsp black pepper
- 1/2 tsp sea salt
- 1 tbsp lemon juice
- 1/4 cup [60ml] unsweetened plain plant-based yogurt
- 2 tbsp chopped fresh cilantro

Directions:
1. Preheat the air fryer to 375°F [190°C].
2. In a small bowl, whisk together the olive oil, turmeric, cumin, smoked paprika, black pepper, sea salt, lemon juice, and plant-based yogurt to create a creamy marinade.
3. Gently brush the marinade over both sides of the cauliflower slabs, ensuring full coverage.
4. Carefully place the slabs in the air fryer basket, ensuring they do not overlap.
5. Air fry for 25 minutes, flipping the slabs carefully at the 15-minute mark to ensure even browning.
6. Garnish with the chopped cilantro before serving.

Lentil-Rice Patties with Avocado Drizzle

Time: 40 minutes	Serving Size: 2 servings
Prep Time: 15 minutes	Cook Time: 25 minutes

Each Serving Has:
Calories: 310, Carbohydrates: 34g, Saturated Fat: 2g, Protein: 12g, Fat: 16g, Sodium: 340mg, Potassium: 780mg, Fiber: 11g, Sugar: 3g, Vitamin C: 20mg, Calcium: 80mg, Iron: 3.2mg

Ingredients:
- 1/2 cup [100g] cooked green lentils, rinsed and drained
- 1/2 cup [90g] cooked brown rice, cooled
- 1/4 cup [40g] chopped red bell pepper
- 1/4 cup [30g] grated carrot
- 2 tbsp chopped fresh cilantro
- 1 tbsp ground flaxseed
- 2 tbsp water
- 1 tbsp olive oil
- 1/2 tsp ground cumin
- 1/4 tsp black pepper
- 1/2 large [75g] mashed ripe avocado
- 2 tbsp lemon juice
- 2 tbsp water
- 1/4 tsp sea salt

Directions:
1. Preheat the air fryer to 375°F [190°C].
2. In a small bowl, combine the ground flaxseed and water to create a flax "egg". Let it sit for 5 minutes until gel-like.
3. In a bowl, mix the cooked lentils, brown rice, chopped bell pepper, cilantro, grated carrot, flax "egg", olive oil, cumin, and black pepper.
4. Mash the mixture until it holds with some texture, then form into 4 equal patties.
5. Arrange the patties in a single layer in the air fryer basket.
6. Air fry for 12 minutes, flip gently, then cook 8–10 more minutes until golden and crisp.
7. Meanwhile, whisk mashed avocado, lemon juice, water, and sea salt in a bowl, adding more water if needed to adjust consistency.
8. Serve the patties warm, drizzled with the avocado sauce.

CHAPTER 5: DINNERS

Tofu Stuffed Portobello Caps

⏱ Time: 35 minutes	🍽 Serving Size: 2 servings
🥗 Prep Time: 15 minutes	👨‍🍳 Cook Time: 20 minutes

Each Serving Has:
Calories: 280, Carbohydrates: 16g, Saturated Fat: 2g, Protein: 18g, Fat: 18g, Sodium: 360mg, Potassium: 860mg, Fiber: 5g, Sugar: 4g, Vitamin C: 22mg, Calcium: 180mg, Iron: 3.5mg

Ingredients:
- 2 large [200g] cleaned Portobello mushroom caps, stems removed
- 1/2 cup [120g] crumbled firm tofu, pressed
- 1/2 cup [80g] chopped spinach
- 1/4 cup [40g] chopped sun-dried tomatoes, rehydrated
- 1/4 cup [30g] chopped red bell pepper
- 2 tbsp nutritional yeast
- 1 tbsp olive oil
- 1/2 tsp garlic powder
- 1/2 tsp dried oregano
- 1/4 tsp smoked paprika
- 1/4 tsp sea salt
- 1/4 tsp black pepper

Directions:
1. Preheat the air fryer to 375°F [190°C].
2. In a medium bowl, combine the crumbled tofu, chopped spinach, sun-dried tomatoes, bell pepper, nutritional yeast, olive oil, garlic powder, oregano, smoked paprika, sea salt, and black pepper. Mix thoroughly to form a cohesive stuffing.
3. Divide the stuffing mixture evenly and spoon it into the cleaned Portobello caps, pressing gently to compact the mixture.
4. Arrange the stuffed caps in a single layer in the air fryer basket.
5. Air fry for 15–20 minutes until the mushrooms are tender and the tops are golden brown.
6. Remove the Portobello caps from the air fryer and serve.

Roasted Pepper Rice Cakes

⏱ Time: 35 minutes	🍽 Serving Size: 2 servings
🥗 Prep Time: 15 minutes	👨‍🍳 Cook Time: 20 minutes

Each Serving Has:
Calories: 310, Carbohydrates: 42g, Saturated Fat: 1g, Protein: 9g, Fat: 10g, Sodium: 300mg, Potassium: 550mg, Fiber: 6g, Sugar: 5g, Vitamin C: 65mg, Calcium: 55mg, Iron: 3mg

Ingredients:
- 1 cup [150g] cooked brown rice, cooled
- 1/2 cup [100g] chopped roasted red bell pepper
- 1/4 cup [60g] mashed cooked chickpeas
- 1/4 cup [30g] chopped fresh parsley
- 2 tbsp chopped green onions
- 2 tbsp ground flaxseed
- 2 tbsp water
- 1 tbsp olive oil
- 1/2 tsp smoked paprika
- 1/4 tsp black pepper
- 1/4 tsp sea salt

Directions:
1. Preheat the air fryer to 375°F [190°C].
2. In a small bowl, combine the ground flaxseed and water to create a flax "egg". Let it sit for 5 minutes to thicken.
3. In a bowl, combine the cooked brown rice, chopped bell pepper, parsley, green onions, mashed chickpeas, olive oil, smoked paprika, sea salt, and black pepper.
4. Add the prepared flax "egg" to the mixture and stir thoroughly until the mixture forms a cohesive texture.
5. Form the mixture into 4 equal-sized patties, pressing firmly to compact them.
6. Arrange the patties in a single layer in the air fryer basket.
7. Air fry for 18–20 minutes, flipping carefully at the halfway mark to ensure even crisping.
8. Remove the cakes from the air fryer and serve.

Pumpkin-Spinach Air-Fry Casserole

Time: 40 minutes
Serving Size: 2 servings
Prep Time: 15 minutes
Cook Time: 25 minutes

Each Serving Has:
Calories: 310, Carbohydrates: 38g, Saturated Fat: 1g, Protein: 10g, Fat: 12g, Sodium: 340mg, Potassium: 720mg, Fiber: 8g, Sugar: 5g, Vitamin C: 19mg, Calcium: 85mg, Iron: 3.4mg

Ingredients:
- 1 cup [240g] mashed cooked pumpkin
- 2 cups [60g] loosely packed fresh spinach leaves
- 1/2 cup [100g] cooked quinoa
- 1/2 cup [120ml] low-sodium vegetable broth
- 1/4 cup [30g] chopped red bell pepper
- 1/4 cup [40g] chopped yellow onion
- 1 tbsp olive oil (+ 1/2 tsp extra for brushing)
- 1/2 tsp garlic powder
- 1/2 tsp smoked paprika
- 1/4 tsp ground nutmeg
- 1/4 tsp sea salt

Directions:
1. Preheat the air fryer to 375°F [190°C].
2. In a skillet over medium heat, sauté the chopped bell pepper and onion with olive oil until softened, about 3-4 minutes.
3. In a bowl, combine the mashed pumpkin, sautéed vegetables, cooked quinoa, garlic powder, smoked paprika, nutmeg, and sea salt. Mix thoroughly until a thick, cohesive mixture forms.
4. Gently fold in the spinach leaves until evenly distributed.
5. Grease two small, oven-safe casserole dishes or ramekins with olive oil. Divide the mixture among the dishes, pressing down slightly to compact.
6. Place the dishes in the air fryer basket. Cook for 25 minutes, or until the tops are golden and slightly crispy.
7. Let the casserole cool for 5 minutes before serving.

Chapter 6: Desserts

Air-Fried Date-Nut Bars

Time: 35 minutes	**Serving Size:** 2 servings
Prep Time: 15 minutes	**Cook Time:** 20 minutes

Each Serving Has:
Calories: 292, Carbohydrates: 42g, Saturated Fat: 1g, Protein: 5g, Fat: 13g, Sodium: 3mg, Potassium: 460mg, Fiber: 6g, Sugar: 27g, Vitamin C: 0.4mg, Calcium: 45mg, Iron: 1.4mg

Ingredients:
- 1/2 cup [90g] pitted Medjool dates
- 1/3 cup [35g] raw walnuts
- 1/3 cup [35g] raw almonds
- 1/4 cup [20g] rolled oats
- 1 tbsp ground flaxseed
- 1/2 tsp ground cinnamon
- 1/4 tsp ground ginger
- 1/4 tsp vanilla extract
- 1 tbsp water

Directions:
1. Preheat the air fryer to 325°F [165°C].
2. In a food processor, combine the pitted dates, walnuts, almonds, oats, ground flaxseed, cinnamon, ginger, vanilla extract, and water.
3. Pulse the mixture until it forms a sticky, coarse dough that holds together when pressed.
4. Line a small, oven-safe baking dish or ramekin with parchment paper. Press the mixture evenly into the bottom, about 1/2 inch [1.25cm] thick.
5. Place the dish into the air fryer basket. Cook for 20 minutes, or until firm and lightly golden on the edges.
6. Let the bake cool for 10 minutes, then lift out and cut into bars.

Crispy Banana Oat Crumble

🕐 Time: 30 minutes	🍽 Serving Size: 2 servings
🥗 Prep Time: 10 minutes	👨‍🍳 Cook Time: 20 minutes

Each Serving Has:
Calories: 285, Carbohydrates: 45g, Saturated Fat: 1g, Protein: 6g, Fat: 10g, Sodium: 5mg, Potassium: 490mg, Fiber: 7g, Sugar: 18g, Vitamin C: 9mg, Calcium: 45mg, Iron: 1.5mg

Ingredients:
- 2 medium [240g] ripe bananas, sliced
- 1/2 cup [50g] rolled oats
- 1/4 cup [30g] chopped raw walnuts
- 2 tbsp unsweetened shredded coconut
- 1 tbsp ground flaxseed
- 1/2 tsp ground cinnamon
- 1/4 tsp ground nutmeg
- 1 tbsp maple syrup (optional)
- 1 tbsp melted coconut oil

Directions:
1. Preheat the air fryer to 350°F [175°C].
2. In a medium bowl, combine the sliced bananas, cinnamon, and nutmeg. Gently toss to coat the bananas evenly.
3. In a separate bowl, mix oats, chopped walnuts, shredded coconut, ground flaxseed, and melted coconut oil. Stir until the mixture forms a crumbly texture.
4. If desired, drizzle maple syrup over the crumble mixture and mix again for added sweetness.
5. In two small oven-safe ramekins or a small baking dish lined with parchment paper, layer the spiced banana slices evenly. Top with the oat crumble mixture, pressing it lightly to form a cohesive layer on top.
6. Place the ramekins or dish into the air fryer basket. Air-fry for 20 minutes, or until the top is golden brown and crispy.
7. Let the crumble cool for 5 minutes before serving.

Sweet Apple Lentil Muffins

🕐 Time: 40 minutes	🍽 Serving Size: 2 servings
🥗 Prep Time: 15 minutes	👨‍🍳 Cook Time: 25 minutes

Each Serving Has:
Calories: 245, Carbohydrates: 38g, Saturated Fat: 1g, Protein: 9g, Fat: 7g, Sodium: 110mg, Potassium: 420mg, Fiber: 7g, Sugar: 12g, Vitamin C: 6mg, Calcium: 70mg, Iron: 2.2mg

Ingredients:
- 1/2 cup [100g] cooked green lentils, cooled
- 1 cup [120g] grated sweet apple, peeled
- 1/2 cup [50g] rolled oats
- 1/4 cup [60ml] unsweetened applesauce
- 1 tbsp ground flaxseed
- 2 tbsp warm water
- 1/2 tsp ground cinnamon
- 1/4 tsp ground nutmeg
- 1/2 tsp baking powder
- 1/4 tsp baking soda
- 1 tbsp maple syrup (optional)
- 1 tbsp melted coconut oil (+ 1/2 tsp extra for brushing)

Directions:
1. Preheat the air fryer to 320°F [160°C].
2. In a small bowl, mix the ground flaxseed and warm water. Let it sit for 5 minutes to form a flax «egg.»
3. In a bowl, combine the cooked lentils, grated apple, oats, applesauce, cinnamon, nutmeg, baking powder, baking soda, and the flax «egg.» Stir well until thick and batter-like.
4. Add the melted coconut oil and maple syrup (if using). Mix again until thoroughly combined.
5. Grease four silicone muffin cups with coconut oil. Divide the batter among them, pressing gently to compact.
6. Place the cups into the air fryer basket. Air-fry for 25 minutes, or until the tops are firm and lightly golden.
7. Let the muffins cool for 5 minutes before removing them from the cups and serving.

CHAPTER 6: DESSERTS

Chocolate Chickpea Crunch Bites

- **Time:** 35 minutes
- **Serving Size:** 2 servings
- **Prep Time:** 10 minutes
- **Cook Time:** 25 minutes

Each Serving Has:
Calories: 220, Carbohydrates: 28g, Saturated Fat: 2g, Protein: 8g, Fat: 9g, Sodium: 110mg, Potassium: 410mg, Fiber: 7g, Sugar: 12g, Vitamin C: 1mg, Calcium: 70mg, Iron: 2.8mg

Ingredients:
- 1 cup [165g] cooked chickpeas, rinsed and patted dry
- 2 tbsp unsweetened cocoa powder
- 2 tbsp maple syrup
- 1/4 cup [20g] rolled oats
- 1/4 cup [30g] chopped raw almonds
- 1/4 cup [60g] mashed ripe banana
- 1 tbsp ground flaxseed
- 2 tbsp warm water
- 1/2 tsp ground cinnamon
- 1/8 tsp sea salt
- 1 tbsp melted coconut oil

Directions:
1. Preheat the air fryer to 350°F [175°C].
2. In a small bowl, combine the ground flaxseed and warm water. Let it sit for 5 minutes to form a flax «egg.»
3. In a mixing bowl, combine the cooked chickpeas, cocoa powder, maple syrup, oats, chopped almonds, mashed banana, cinnamon, sea salt, the prepared flax «egg,» and melted coconut oil. Mash the mixture using a fork or potato masher until it holds together but still has some texture.
4. Using your hands, form the mixture into approximately 10 bite-sized balls.
5. Place the bites in a single layer in the air fryer basket. Air-fry for 25 minutes, shaking the basket halfway through for even crisping.
6. Allow the bites to cool for 5 minutes before serving.

Baked Cinnamon Quinoa Squares

- **Time:** 40 minutes
- **Serving Size:** 2 servings
- **Prep Time:** 10 minutes
- **Cook Time:** 30 minutes

Each Serving Has:
Calories: 210, Carbohydrates: 32g, Saturated Fat: 1.2g, Protein: 6g, Fat: 7g, Sodium: 120mg, Potassium: 290mg, Fiber: 5g, Sugar: 8g, Vitamin C: 1mg, Calcium: 55mg, Iron: 2.1mg

Ingredients:
- 1 cup [185g] cooked quinoa, cooled
- 1/2 cup [120ml] unsweetened almond milk
- 1/4 cup [60g] mashed ripe banana
- 2 tbsp maple syrup
- 1/4 cup [25g] chopped walnuts
- 2 tbsp ground flaxseed
- 1/2 cup [50g] rolled oats
- 1 tsp ground cinnamon
- 1/4 tsp ground nutmeg
- 1/2 tsp baking powder
- 1/8 tsp sea salt
- 1 tsp vanilla extract

Directions:
1. Preheat the air fryer to 325°F [165°C].
2. In a small bowl, combine the ground flaxseed and almond milk to form a flax «egg.» Let it rest for 5 minutes.
3. In a larger bowl, mix the cooked quinoa, mashed banana, maple syrup, chopped walnuts, oats, cinnamon, nutmeg, baking powder, sea salt, and vanilla extract. Stir in the prepared flax «egg» until the mixture forms a cohesive texture.
4. Transfer the mixture into a small square silicone or parchment-lined pan that fits your air fryer basket. Flatten and smooth the top evenly.
5. Air-fry for 30 minutes or until firm and lightly golden on top.
6. Allow the dish to cool for 5–10 minutes, then cut into 4 squares.

Coconut-Carrot Pudding Cups

- **Time:** 35 minutes
- **Serving Size:** 2 servings
- **Prep Time:** 10 minutes
- **Cook Time:** 25 minutes

Each Serving Has:
Calories: 248, Carbohydrates: 33g, Saturated Fat: 6.1g, Protein: 5g, Fat: 10g, Sodium: 123mg, Potassium: 431mg, Fiber: 5g, Sugar: 12g, Vitamin C: 4mg, Calcium: 59mg, Iron: 1.9mg

Ingredients:
- 1 cup [120g] grated carrot
- 1/4 cup [45g] rinsed cooked red lentils
- 1/2 cup [120ml] unsweetened coconut milk
- 1 tbsp maple syrup
- 2 tbsp unsweetened shredded coconut
- 1/4 cup [25g] rolled oats
- 1/2 tsp ground cinnamon
- 1/8 tsp ground cardamom
- 1/2 tsp vanilla extract
- 1/4 tsp sea salt

Directions:
1. Preheat the air fryer to 350°F [175°C].
2. In a mixing bowl, combine the grated carrot, cooked lentils, and oats.
3. Stir in the coconut milk, maple syrup, shredded coconut, cinnamon, cardamom, vanilla extract, and sea salt. Mix until evenly incorporated and thick.
4. Divide the mixture evenly into two small ramekins or silicone muffin molds that fit your air fryer basket. Smooth the tops with a spoon.
5. Place the ramekins into the air fryer basket and air-fry for 25 minutes, or until set and lightly golden on top.
6. Let the pudding cups cool for 5 minutes before serving warm.

Peanut Butter Apple Wedges

- **Time:** 20 minutes
- **Serving Size:** 2 servings
- **Prep Time:** 10 minutes
- **Cook Time:** 10 minutes

Each Serving Has:
Calories: 210, Carbohydrates: 29g, Saturated Fat: 1.5g, Protein: 5g, Fat: 9g, Sodium: 75mg, Potassium: 295mg, Fiber: 5g, Sugar: 18g, Vitamin C: 6mg, Calcium: 35mg, Iron: 1mg

Ingredients:
- 1 large [200g] crisp apple, cored and cut into wedges
- 2 tbsp creamy natural peanut butter
- 1/4 cup [20g] rolled oats
- 1/2 tsp ground cinnamon
- 1 tsp maple syrup
- 1/4 tsp sea salt

Directions:
1. Preheat the air fryer to 350°F [175°C].
2. In a small bowl, combine the oats, cinnamon, maple syrup, and sea salt until the oats are well-coated.
3. Spread the peanut butter evenly over each apple wedge.
4. Press the oat mixture gently onto the peanut butter-coated sides of the apple wedges to create a crunchy layer.
5. Arrange the apple wedges in a single layer in the air fryer basket.
6. Air-fry for 10 minutes until the oat layer is golden and the apples are slightly softened.
7. Remove the apple wedges from the air fryer and serve warm.

Air-Fried Berry-Filled Oat Discs

- **Time:** 25 minutes
- **Serving Size:** 2 servings
- **Prep Time:** 10 minutes
- **Cook Time:** 15 minutes

Each Serving Has:
Calories: 230, Carbohydrates: 34g, Saturated Fat: 1.5g, Protein: 6g, Fat: 8g, Sodium: 85mg, Potassium: 310mg, Fiber: 6g, Sugar: 12g, Vitamin C: 9mg, Calcium: 40mg, Iron: 2mg

Ingredients:
- 1 cup [90g] rolled oats
- 1/4 cup [60ml] unsweetened almond milk
- 1/2 cup [75g] mixed fresh berries (blueberries, raspberries, or chopped strawberries)
- 2 tbsp almond butter
- 1 tbsp maple syrup
- 1/2 tsp ground cinnamon
- 1/8 tsp sea salt
- 1 tsp chia seeds

Directions:
1. Preheat the air fryer to 350°F [175°C].
2. In a mixing bowl, combine the oats, almond milk, almond butter, maple syrup, cinnamon, sea salt, and chia seeds. Stir well until the mixture thickens slightly.
3. Scoop 2 tablespoons of the oat mixture into your hand, flatten into a disc, and place one tablespoon of mixed berries in the center. Top with another tablespoon of oat mixture, sealing the edges to form a filled disc. Repeat for the remaining mixture.
4. Arrange the discs in a single layer in the air fryer basket.
5. Air-fry for 15 minutes, flipping them gently at the 8-minute mark to ensure even crisping.
6. Remove the oat discs from the air fryer and serve.

Roasted Pear and Almond Rounds

- **Time:** 22 minutes
- **Serving Size:** 2 servings
- **Prep Time:** 7 minutes
- **Cook Time:** 15 minutes

Each Serving Has:
Calories: 210, Carbohydrates: 28g, Saturated Fat: 1.2g, Protein: 4g, Fat: 10g, Sodium: 45mg, Potassium: 310mg, Fiber: 5g, Sugar: 18g, Vitamin C: 8mg, Calcium: 50mg, Iron: 1.4mg

Ingredients:
- 1 large [200g] firm ripe pear, cored and sliced into 8 rounds
- 2 tbsp almond butter
- 2 tbsp chopped raw almonds
- 1 tbsp unsweetened shredded coconut
- 1/2 tsp ground cinnamon
- 1/4 tsp ground nutmeg
- 1/8 tsp sea salt
- 1/2 tsp maple syrup (optional)

Directions:
1. Preheat the air fryer to 360°F [182°C].
2. In a small bowl, combine the almond butter, cinnamon, nutmeg, sea salt, and maple syrup (if using). Mix into a smooth paste.
3. Spread the almond butter mixture evenly on four pear slices, then top each with the remaining pear slices to form sandwich-style rounds.
4. Sprinkle the tops with the chopped almonds and shredded coconut, pressing lightly so they stick.
5. Arrange the rounds in a single layer in the air fryer basket.
6. Air-fry for 15 minutes, checking at the 10-minute mark to prevent over-browning.
7. Remove the pear rounds from the air fryer and serve warm.

Pumpkin-Chia Spice Cookies

Time: 30 minutes
Serving Size: 2 servings
Prep Time: 10 minutes
Cook Time: 20 minutes

Each Serving Has:
Calories: 235, Carbohydrates: 32g, Saturated Fat: 1g, Protein: 6g, Fat: 9g, Sodium: 135mg, Potassium: 310mg, Fiber: 7g, Sugar: 10g, Vitamin C: 5mg, Calcium: 90mg, Iron: 2.4mg

Ingredients:
- 1/2 cup [120g] unsweetened pumpkin purée
- 1/3 cup [30g] rolled oats, ground into flour
- 2 tbsp chia seeds
- 2 tbsp almond flour
- 2 tbsp maple syrup
- 1/2 tsp ground cinnamon
- 1/4 tsp ground nutmeg
- 1/4 tsp ground ginger
- 1/8 tsp sea salt
- 1/2 tsp vanilla extract

Directions:
1. Preheat the air fryer to 340°F [170°C].
2. In a medium mixing bowl, combine the pumpkin purée, maple syrup, and vanilla extract, stirring until smooth.
3. Add the ground oats, chia seeds, almond flour, cinnamon, nutmeg, ginger, and sea salt. Mix until a thick, cohesive dough forms.
4. Scoop out the mixture and shape it into small balls, flattening them slightly to form cookie discs.
5. Arrange the cookies in a single layer in the air fryer basket, ensuring they do not touch.
6. Air-fry for 20 minutes, flipping them gently after 10 minutes for even cooking.
7. Let the cookies cool for 5 minutes before serving.

Maple-Glazed Sweet Potato Coins

Time: 30 minutes
Serving Size: 2 servings
Prep Time: 10 minutes
Cook Time: 20 minutes

Each Serving Has:
Calories: 210, Carbohydrates: 38g, Saturated Fat: 0.5g, Protein: 2g, Fat: 5g, Sodium: 120mg, Potassium: 450mg, Fiber: 5g, Sugar: 15g, Vitamin C: 12mg, Calcium: 50mg, Iron: 1.2mg

Ingredients:
- 2 cups [300g] peeled and sliced sweet potato, cut into 1/4-inch thick coins
- 1 tbsp maple syrup
- 1 tsp olive oil
- 1/2 tsp ground cinnamon
- 1/4 tsp ground nutmeg
- 1/4 tsp sea salt

Directions:
1. Preheat the air fryer to 375°F [190°C].
2. In a mixing bowl, combine the sweet potato coins with maple syrup, olive oil, cinnamon, nutmeg, and sea salt. Toss until the coins are evenly coated with the mixture.
3. Arrange the sweet potato coins in a single layer in the air fryer basket, ensuring they don't overlap.
4. Air-fry for 20 minutes, flipping the coins gently at the 10-minute mark for even caramelization.
5. Serve warm, optionally drizzling with any remaining glaze from the bowl.

Mango Coconut Rice Puffs

Time: 35 minutes
Serving Size: 2 servings
Prep Time: 15 minutes
Cook Time: 20 minutes

Each Serving Has:
Calories: 230, Carbohydrates: 38g, Saturated Fat: 5g, Protein: 4g, Fat: 7g, Sodium: 105mg, Potassium: 280mg, Fiber: 4g, Sugar: 15g, Vitamin C: 20mg, Calcium: 45mg, Iron: 1.6mg

Ingredients:
- 1 cup [200g] cooked and cooled brown rice
- 1/2 cup [80g] diced ripe mango
- 1/4 cup [20g] unsweetened shredded coconut
- 1 tbsp chia seeds
- 1 tbsp maple syrup
- 1/2 tsp ground cinnamon
- 1/8 tsp sea salt
- 1 tsp coconut oil (optional)

Directions:
1. Preheat the air fryer to 350°F [175°C].
2. In a mixing bowl, combine the cooked brown rice, diced mango, shredded coconut, chia seeds, maple syrup, cinnamon, and sea salt. Mix until a sticky, cohesive mixture forms.
3. Scoop out portions of the mixture and shape into small, bite-sized discs using your hands.
4. Lightly grease the air fryer basket with coconut oil or use parchment paper liners. Arrange the rice puffs in the air fryer basket in a single layer without overcrowding.
5. Air-fry for 20 minutes, flipping the puffs carefully halfway through to ensure even crisping.
6. Remove the puffs from the air fryer and serve.

Banana-Cocoa Mini Cakes

Time: 30 minutes
Serving Size: 2 servings
Prep Time: 10 minutes
Cook Time: 20 minutes

Each Serving Has:
Calories: 210, Carbohydrates: 36g, Saturated Fat: 2g, Protein: 5g, Fat: 7g, Sodium: 140mg, Potassium: 450mg, Fiber: 5g, Sugar: 16g, Vitamin C: 8mg, Calcium: 60mg, Iron: 2mg

Ingredients:
- 1 large [120g] mashed ripe banana
- 1/2 cup [50g] rolled oats, ground into flour
- 2 tbsp unsweetened cocoa powder
- 1/4 cup [60ml] unsweetened almond milk
- 1 tbsp chia seeds
- 1 tbsp maple syrup
- 1/2 tsp baking powder
- 1/4 tsp ground cinnamon
- 1/8 tsp sea salt

Directions:
1. Preheat the air fryer to 350°F [175°C].
2. In a mixing bowl, combine the mashed banana, oat flour, cocoa powder, almond milk, chia seeds, maple syrup, baking powder, cinnamon, and sea salt. Mix thoroughly until a smooth, thick batter forms.
3. Spoon the batter evenly into two silicone muffin cups or small ramekins.
4. Place the cups in the air fryer basket and cook for 20 minutes, checking for doneness with a toothpick inserted into the center (it should come out clean).
5. Let the mini cakes cool for 5 minutes before serving.

Orange-Date Bliss Squares

⏲ Time: 30 minutes	🍽 Serving Size: 2 servings
🥗 Prep Time: 10 minutes	👨‍🍳 Cook Time: 20 minutes

Each Serving Has:
Calories: 220, Carbohydrates: 38g, Saturated Fat: 2g, Protein: 5g, Fat: 7g, Sodium: 80mg, Potassium: 480mg, Fiber: 6g, Sugar: 22g, Vitamin C: 15mg, Calcium: 65mg, Iron: 2.1mg

Ingredients:
- 1/2 cup [75g] pitted, chopped Medjool dates
- 1/2 cup [120ml] orange juice
- 1/2 cup [50g] rolled oats, ground into flour
- 1/4 cup [60ml] unsweetened almond milk
- 2 tbsp unsweetened shredded coconut
- 1 tbsp chia seeds
- 1/2 tsp ground cinnamon
- 1/4 tsp orange zest
- 1/8 tsp sea salt

Directions:
1. Preheat the air fryer to 350°F [175°C].
2. In a small saucepan, simmer the chopped dates in orange juice over low heat for 3–4 minutes, stirring until the dates soften and a thick paste forms. Remove from heat and let cool slightly.
3. In a mixing bowl, combine the oat flour, almond milk, shredded coconut, chia seeds, cinnamon, orange zest, and sea salt. Stir in the cooled date mixture until a thick, sticky dough forms.
4. Press the dough evenly into two small silicone molds or ramekins to shape into squares.
5. Place the molds in the air fryer basket and cook for 20 minutes.
6. Allow the bliss squares to cool for 5 minutes before removing from the molds and serving.

Air-Fried Almond-Cinnamon Twists

⏲ Time: 28 minutes	🍽 Serving Size: 2 servings
🥗 Prep Time: 10 minutes	👨‍🍳 Cook Time: 18 minutes

Each Serving Has:
Calories: 198, Carbohydrates: 25g, Saturated Fat: 1g, Protein: 6g, Fat: 8g, Sodium: 92mg, Potassium: 255mg, Fiber: 5g, Sugar: 7g, Vitamin C: 0.4mg, Calcium: 92mg, Iron: 1.6mg

Ingredients:
- 1/2 cup [80g] mashed ripe banana
- 1/2 cup [45g] rolled oats, ground into flour
- 1/4 cup [25g] ground almonds
- 1 tbsp maple syrup
- 1 tbsp almond butter
- 1/2 tsp ground cinnamon
- 1/4 tsp baking powder
- 1/8 tsp sea salt

Directions:
1. Preheat the air fryer to 350°F [175°C].
2. In a mixing bowl, combine the mashed banana, maple syrup, and almond butter until smooth.
3. Stir in the oat flour, ground almonds, cinnamon, baking powder, and sea salt until a thick dough forms.
4. Divide the dough in half and roll each portion into a rope about 6 inches [15cm] long. Twist each rope into a spiral or helical shape and lightly press to flatten it.
5. Place the twists in the air fryer basket, lined with parchment or a silicone mat.
6. Air fry for 18 minutes, flipping the twists once halfway through, until golden and slightly crisp on the outside.
7. Let the twists cool for 5 minutes before serving.

CHAPTER 6: DESSERTS ◊ 81

Apricot-Oat Tartlets

⏲ Time: 30 minutes	🍽 Serving Size: 2 servings
🥗 Prep Time: 10 minutes	👨‍🍳 Cook Time: 20 minutes

Each Serving Has:
Calories: 215, Carbohydrates: 32g, Saturated Fat: 1g, Protein: 5g, Fat: 8g, Sodium: 90mg, Potassium: 290mg, Fiber: 6g, Sugar: 14g, Vitamin C: 3mg, Calcium: 75mg, Iron: 1.8mg

Ingredients:
- 1/2 cup [45g] rolled oats, ground into flour
- 1/4 cup [30g] chopped dried apricots
- 2 tbsp maple syrup
- 1 tbsp almond butter
- 1/4 tsp ground cinnamon
- 1/4 cup [60ml] unsweetened almond milk
- 1/2 tsp baking powder
- 1/8 tsp sea salt
- 1/4 tsp vanilla extract

Directions:
1. Preheat the air fryer to 350°F [175°C].
2. In a mixing bowl, combine the oat flour, chopped apricots, cinnamon, baking powder, and sea salt.
3. In a separate small bowl, whisk together the almond butter, maple syrup, almond milk, and vanilla extract until smooth.
4. Pour the wet mixture into the dry ingredients and stir until a thick batter forms.
5. Divide the batter evenly into two silicone muffin molds or ramekins, gently pressing down to flatten the tops.
6. Place the molds in the air fryer basket.
7. Air fry for 20 minutes, checking for a lightly golden top and firm texture.
8. Allow the tartlets to cool for 5 minutes before removing from the molds and serving.

Stuffed Baked Figs with Walnuts

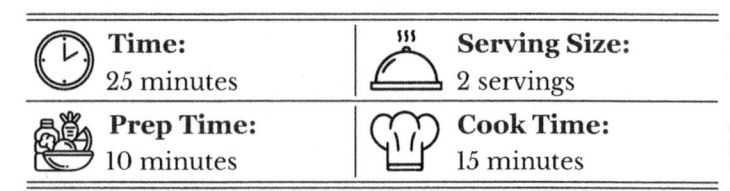

⏲ Time: 25 minutes	🍽 Serving Size: 2 servings
🥗 Prep Time: 10 minutes	👨‍🍳 Cook Time: 15 minutes

Each Serving Has:
Calories: 210, Carbohydrates: 29g, Saturated Fat: 1g, Protein: 4g, Fat: 10g, Sodium: 5mg, Potassium: 370mg, Fiber: 5g, Sugar: 21g, Vitamin C: 2mg, Calcium: 60mg, Iron: 1.2mg

Ingredients:
- 6 medium fresh figs, halved
- 1/4 cup [30g] chopped raw walnuts
- 1 tbsp maple syrup
- 1/2 tsp ground cinnamon
- 1/4 tsp ground nutmeg
- 1/4 tsp vanilla extract
- 1/8 tsp sea salt

Directions:
1. Preheat the air fryer to 350°F [175°C].
2. In a small mixing bowl, combine the chopped walnuts, maple syrup, cinnamon, nutmeg, vanilla extract, and sea salt to form a sticky filling.
3. Gently open the halved figs and spoon the walnut mixture evenly into the center of each half.
4. Arrange the stuffed figs in a single layer in the air fryer basket.
5. Air fry for 15 minutes, until the figs are tender and the walnut filling is golden and slightly crisp.
6. Allow the figs to cool slightly before serving.

Apple-Raisin Oat Rounds

- **Time:** 30 minutes
- **Serving Size:** 2 servings
- **Prep Time:** 10 minutes
- **Cook Time:** 20 minutes

Each Serving Has:
Calories: 230, Carbohydrates: 35g, Saturated Fat: 1g, Protein: 5g, Fat: 8g, Sodium: 45mg, Potassium: 290mg, Fiber: 5g, Sugar: 14g, Vitamin C: 4mg, Calcium: 50mg, Iron: 1.4mg

Ingredients:
- 1 cup [100g] rolled oats
- 1/2 cup [75g] grated sweet apple
- 1/4 cup [40g] raisins
- 2 tbsp unsweetened applesauce
- 1 tbsp maple syrup
- 1 tbsp ground flaxseed
- 1/2 tsp ground cinnamon
- 1/4 tsp ground nutmeg
- 1/4 tsp sea salt
- 1/4 tsp baking powder

Directions:
1. Preheat the air fryer to 350°F [175°C].
2. In a mixing bowl, combine the oats, grated apple, raisins, applesauce, maple syrup, ground flaxseed, cinnamon, nutmeg, sea salt, and baking powder. Mix thoroughly until a sticky dough forms.
3. Using your hands, shape the mixture into 6 equal-sized rounds and flatten them slightly to form discs.
4. Arrange the oat rounds in a single layer in the air fryer basket.
5. Air fry for 20 minutes, flipping the rounds carefully at the 10-minute mark for even crisping.
6. Allow the oat rounds to cool slightly before serving.

Ginger Beet Cookie Slices

- **Time:** 30 minutes
- **Serving Size:** 2 servings
- **Prep Time:** 10 minutes
- **Cook Time:** 20 minutes

Each Serving Has:
Calories: 210, Carbohydrates: 34g, Saturated Fat: 1g, Protein: 4g, Fat: 7g, Sodium: 55mg, Potassium: 310mg, Fiber: 5g, Sugar: 12g, Vitamin C: 3mg, Calcium: 45mg, Iron: 1.6mg

Ingredients:
- 1/2 cup [75g] grated cooked beet, cooled
- 1/2 cup [50g] rolled oats
- 1/4 cup [30g] almond flour
- 2 tbsp unsweetened applesauce
- 2 tbsp chopped soft dates
- 1 tbsp ground flaxseed
- 1/2 tsp ground ginger
- 1/4 tsp ground cinnamon
- 1/4 tsp baking powder
- 1/8 tsp sea salt

Directions:
1. Preheat the air fryer to 350°F [175°C].
2. In a mixing bowl, combine the grated cooked beet, oats, almond flour, applesauce, chopped dates, ground flaxseed, ginger, cinnamon, baking powder, and sea salt. Stir until a thick, slightly sticky dough forms.
3. Divide the dough and shape into six small discs or oval slices using your hands. Flatten them slightly to form even, cookie-shaped pieces.
4. Place the cookie slices in a single layer in the air fryer basket, ensuring they do not touch.
5. Air fry for 20 minutes, flipping gently after 10 minutes for even crisping.
6. Let the cookie slices cool for 5 minutes before serving.

CHAPTER 6: DESSERTS

Vanilla Millet Pudding Puffs

Time: 45 minutes
Serving Size: 2 servings
Prep Time: 15 minutes
Cook Time: 30 minutes

Each Serving Has:
Calories: 215, Carbohydrates: 36g, Saturated Fat: 1g, Protein: 6g, Fat: 6g, Sodium: 55mg, Potassium: 210mg, Fiber: 4g, Sugar: 8g, Vitamin C: 1mg, Calcium: 45mg, Iron: 2.1mg

Ingredients:
- 1/2 cup [100g] cooked and cooled millet
- 1/4 cup [60ml] unsweetened almond milk
- 2 tbsp mashed ripe banana
- 2 tbsp chopped dried apricots
- 1 tbsp ground flaxseed
- 1 tbsp maple syrup
- 1 tsp vanilla extract
- 1/2 tsp ground cinnamon
- 1/4 tsp ground nutmeg
- 1/4 tsp baking powder
- 1/8 tsp sea salt

Directions:
1. Preheat the air fryer to 350°F [175°C].
2. In a mixing bowl, combine the cooked millet, almond milk, mashed banana, chopped apricots, ground flaxseed, maple syrup, vanilla extract, cinnamon, nutmeg, baking powder, and sea salt. Stir well until a thick, cohesive batter forms.
3. Using your hands or a spoon, shape the mixture into small round puffs, about the size of a golf ball. Flatten slightly to create a puffed disc shape.
4. Arrange the puffs in a single layer in the air fryer basket, ensuring space between them for even airflow.
5. Air fry for 30 minutes, flipping gently at the 15-minute mark for uniform crispness.
6. Let the puffs cool for 5 minutes before serving.

Cinnamon-Roasted Carrot Bars

Time: 40 minutes
Serving Size: 2 servings
Prep Time: 15 minutes
Cook Time: 25 minutes

Each Serving Has:
Calories: 198, Carbohydrates: 34g, Saturated Fat: 1g, Protein: 4g, Fat: 6g, Sodium: 62mg, Potassium: 370mg, Fiber: 5g, Sugar: 14g, Vitamin C: 3mg, Calcium: 47mg, Iron: 1.4mg

Ingredients:
- 1 cup [120g] grated raw carrot
- 1/2 cup [50g] rolled oats
- 1/4 cup [60ml] unsweetened applesauce
- 2 tbsp chopped raw walnuts
- 2 tbsp raisins
- 1 tbsp ground flaxseed
- 1 tbsp maple syrup
- 1/2 tsp ground cinnamon
- 1/4 tsp ground ginger
- 1/4 tsp baking powder
- 1/8 tsp sea salt

Directions:
1. Preheat the air fryer to 350°F [175°C].
2. In a mixing bowl, combine the grated carrot, oats, applesauce, chopped walnuts, raisins, ground flaxseed, maple syrup, cinnamon, ginger, baking powder, and sea salt. Stir until thoroughly combined into a thick mixture.
3. Line a small air fryer-safe baking dish or ramekin with parchment paper. Press the mixture evenly into the dish to form a compact layer about 3/4 inch thick.
4. Place the dish in the air fryer basket and cook for 25 minutes, or until the top is firm and golden brown.
5. Let it cool for 5 minutes before slicing into bars.

Tahini-Date Energy Donuts

⏲ Time: 35 minutes	🍽 Serving Size: 2 servings
🥗 Prep Time: 15 minutes	👨‍🍳 Cook Time: 20 minutes

Each Serving Has:
Calories: 212, Carbohydrates: 33g, Saturated Fat: 1g, Protein: 5g, Fat: 8g, Sodium: 48mg, Potassium: 346mg, Fiber: 5g, Sugar: 20g, Vitamin C: 0mg, Calcium: 72mg, Iron: 1.8mg

Ingredients:
- 1/2 cup [90g] pitted, chopped Medjool dates
- 1/4 cup [60ml] warm water
- 1/3 cup [30g] rolled oats
- 2 tbsp smooth tahini
- 1 tbsp ground flaxseed
- 1/2 tsp ground cinnamon
- 1/4 tsp ground ginger
- 1/4 tsp baking powder
- 1/8 tsp sea salt

Directions:
1. Preheat the air fryer to 350°F [175°C].
2. In a small bowl, soak the chopped dates in warm water for 10 minutes, until they are softened.
3. In a food processor, combine the soaked dates with their soaking water, oats, smooth tahini, ground flaxseed, cinnamon, ginger, baking powder, and sea salt. Blend until a sticky dough forms.
4. Using damp hands, shape the dough into two donut-shaped rounds and place them in a silicone donut mold or on a parchment-lined small tray that fits your air fryer.
5. Air fry for 20 minutes, or until the edges are golden and the donuts are firm to the touch.
6. Let the donuts cool for 5 minutes before removing from the mold and serving.

Chocolate Avocado Truffle Balls

⏲ Time: 30 minutes	🍽 Serving Size: 2 servings
🥗 Prep Time: 20 minutes	👨‍🍳 Cook Time: 10 minutes

Each Serving Has:
Calories: 225, Carbohydrates: 21g, Saturated Fat: 2g, Protein: 5g, Fat: 15g, Sodium: 10mg, Potassium: 530mg, Fiber: 8g, Sugar: 12g, Vitamin C: 9mg, Calcium: 45mg, Iron: 2mg

Ingredients:
- 1/2 cup [120g] mashed ripe avocado
- 1/4 cup [24g] unsweetened cocoa powder
- 1/4 cup [40g] chopped pitted Medjool dates
- 2 tbsp rolled oats
- 1 tbsp maple syrup
- 1/2 tsp vanilla extract
- 1/4 tsp ground cinnamon
- 1/8 tsp sea salt

Directions:
1. Preheat the air fryer to 325°F [160°C].
2. In a mixing bowl, combine the mashed avocado, cocoa powder, chopped dates, oats, maple syrup, vanilla extract, cinnamon, and sea salt. Mix thoroughly until a thick, sticky dough forms.
3. Using slightly damp hands, shape the mixture into small, even balls, approximately the size of a truffle.
4. Place the truffle balls into a parchment-lined air fryer basket, ensuring they don't touch each other.
5. Air fry for 10 minutes, allowing the outer layer to firm slightly while keeping the centers creamy and tender.
6. Let the truffle balls cool for 5 minutes before serving.

Peach-Buckwheat Crisp

⏱ Time: 30 minutes	🍽 Serving Size: 2 servings
🥗 Prep Time: 15 minutes	👨‍🍳 Cook Time: 15 minutes

Each Serving Has:
Calories: 218, Carbohydrates: 40g, Saturated Fat: 1g, Protein: 5g, Fat: 7g, Sodium: 3mg, Potassium: 422mg, Fiber: 6g, Sugar: 17g, Vitamin C: 10mg, Calcium: 28mg, Iron: 2mg

Ingredients:
- 1 cup [150g] thinly sliced ripe peaches
- 1/4 cup [40g] chopped Medjool dates, pitted
- 1/4 tsp ground cinnamon
- 1/4 tsp vanilla extract
- 1/2 cup [80g] cooked buckwheat groats, cooled
- 1/4 cup [20g] rolled oats
- 1 tbsp almond butter
- 1/2 tsp ground flaxseed
- 1/4 tsp ground ginger
- 1/2 tsp lemon juice

Directions:
1. Preheat the air fryer to 350°F [175°C].
2. In a bowl, combine the sliced peaches, chopped dates, cinnamon, vanilla extract, and lemon juice. Toss well to coat the fruit mixture evenly.
3. In a separate bowl, mix the cooked buckwheat groats, oats, almond butter, ground flaxseed, and ginger. Stir until the mixture forms a cohesive, crumbly topping.
4. Spoon the peach-date mixture into two small, oven-safe ramekins or silicone molds suitable for the air fryer.
5. Evenly distribute the buckwheat-oat topping over each ramekin.
6. Place the ramekins in the air fryer basket and cook for 15 minutes, or until the topping is lightly crisp and golden.
7. Let the crisp cool for 5 minutes before serving warm.

Air-Fried Polenta Lemon Wedges

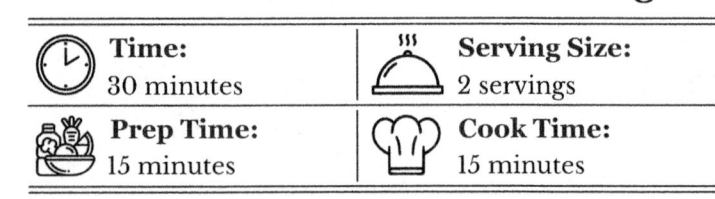

⏱ Time: 30 minutes	🍽 Serving Size: 2 servings
🥗 Prep Time: 15 minutes	👨‍🍳 Cook Time: 15 minutes

Each Serving Has:
Calories: 220, Carbohydrates: 33g, Saturated Fat: 1g, Protein: 3g, Fat: 7g, Sodium: 60mg, Potassium: 140mg, Fiber: 2g, Sugar: 10g, Vitamin C: 7mg, Calcium: 20mg, Iron: 1mg

Ingredients:
- 1 cup [250g] cooked and cooled firm polenta
- 1 tsp lemon zest
- 2 tbsp lemon juice
- 1 tbsp maple syrup
- 1 tbsp melted coconut oil
- 1/2 tsp ground cinnamon
- 2 tbsp coconut sugar
- 1 tbsp chopped fresh mint

Directions:
1. Preheat the air fryer to 375°F [190°C].
2. Cut the cooked firm polenta into 8 equal wedges.
3. In a bowl, combine the lemon zest, lemon juice, maple syrup, coconut oil, cinnamon, and coconut sugar. Mix well to form a bright, sweet glaze.
4. Gently toss the polenta wedges in the glaze, ensuring each wedge is evenly coated.
5. Arrange the coated polenta wedges in a single layer in the air fryer basket.
6. Cook for 15 minutes, flipping the wedges halfway through for even crisping.
7. Sprinkle with the chopped mint before serving.

Pineapple Basil Dessert Skewers

⏰ Time: 20 minutes	🍽 Serving Size: 2 servings
🥗 Prep Time: 10 minutes	👨‍🍳 Cook Time: 10 minutes

Each Serving Has:
Calories: 122, Carbohydrates: 31g, Saturated Fat: 0g, Protein: 1g, Fat: 0.3g, Sodium: 2mg, Potassium: 263mg, Fiber: 2g, Sugar: 24g, Vitamin C: 79mg, Calcium: 21mg, Iron: 0.6mg

Ingredients:
- 1 1/2 cups [240g] cubed ripe pineapple
- 1/2 cup [75g] halved ripe strawberries
- 1 tbsp chopped fresh basil
- 1 tsp lemon juice
- 1/2 tsp ground cinnamon
- 1/2 tsp maple syrup
- 1/4 tsp ground ginger

Directions:
1. Preheat the air fryer to 375°F [190°C].
2. In a bowl, combine the cubed pineapple, halved strawberries, chopped basil, lemon juice, cinnamon, maple syrup, and ginger. Toss gently to coat the fruit evenly.
3. Thread the fruit mixture onto skewers, alternating pineapple and strawberries for a colorful presentation.
4. Arrange the skewers in a single layer in the air fryer basket.
5. Air-fry for 10 minutes, turning the skewers halfway through to ensure even caramelization.
6. Let the skewers cool slightly before serving warm.

Roasted Strawberry Oat Fritters

⏰ Time: 25 minutes	🍽 Serving Size: 2 servings
🥗 Prep Time: 10 minutes	👨‍🍳 Cook Time: 15 minutes

Each Serving Has:
Calories: 210, Carbohydrates: 36g, Saturated Fat: 0.6g, Protein: 5g, Fat: 4g, Sodium: 72mg, Potassium: 315mg, Fiber: 6g, Sugar: 14g, Vitamin C: 49mg, Calcium: 58mg, Iron: 2.1mg

Ingredients:
- 1 cup [90g] rolled oats
- 1/2 cup [80g] chopped fresh strawberries
- 1/4 cup [60ml] unsweetened almond milk
- 2 tbsp mashed ripe banana
- 1 tbsp chia seeds
- 1 tbsp maple syrup
- 1/2 tsp ground cinnamon
- 1/4 tsp ground ginger
- 1/4 tsp sea salt

Directions:
1. Preheat the air fryer to 375°F [190°C].
2. In a mixing bowl, combine the oats, chopped strawberries, mashed banana, chia seeds, maple syrup, cinnamon, ginger, and sea salt. Pour in the almond milk and mix until the ingredients are well incorporated into a thick, sticky batter.
3. Let the mixture rest for 5 minutes, allowing the chia seeds to bind the batter.
4. Form the mixture into small, flat fritters using your hands or a spoon. You should get approximately 4 fritters.
5. Arrange the fritters in a single layer in the air fryer basket.
6. Air-fry for 15 minutes, flipping them halfway through to ensure even crisping.
7. Remove the fritters from the air fryer and serve warm.

Blueberry-Lime Crisp Cubes

⏰ **Time:** 30 minutes	🍽 **Serving Size:** 2 servings
🥗 **Prep Time:** 10 minutes	👨‍🍳 **Cook Time:** 20 minutes

Each Serving Has:
Calories: 210, Carbohydrates: 38g, Saturated Fat: 0.8g, Protein: 5g, Fat: 5g, Sodium: 60mg, Potassium: 310mg, Fiber: 6g, Sugar: 16g, Vitamin C: 18mg, Calcium: 55mg, Iron: 2mg

Ingredients:
- 1 cup [150g] fresh blueberries
- 3/4 cup [70g] rolled oats
- 1/4 cup [60ml] unsweetened almond milk
- 2 tbsp mashed ripe banana
- 1 tbsp maple syrup
- 1 tbsp lime juice
- 1 tsp lime zest
- 1 tbsp chia seeds
- 1/2 tsp ground cinnamon
- 1/4 tsp sea salt

Directions:
1. Preheat the air fryer to 350°F [175°C].
2. In a mixing bowl, combine the blueberries, mashed banana, maple syrup, lime juice, and lime zest. Gently fold in oats, chia seeds, cinnamon, sea salt, and almond milk until a thick, slightly sticky batter forms.
3. Allow the mixture to rest for 5 minutes to activate the chia seeds and allow the batter to thicken.
4. Using your hands or a silicone mold, shape the mixture into compact cubes. You should form approximately 4 cubes.
5. Arrange the cubes in a single layer in the air fryer basket.
6. Air-fry for 20 minutes, flipping the cubes carefully halfway through to achieve even crisping on all sides.
7. Remove the cubes from the air fryer and serve.

Chapter 7: 28-Day Meal Prep Plan

Week	Day	Breakfast	Lunch	Snack or appetizer	Dinner
Week 1:	1	Air-Fried Banana Oat Patties	Air-Fried Falafel Wrap	Crispy Chickpea Snack Bombs	Air-Fried Tofu Steak with Chimichurri
	2	Sweet Potato Breakfast Boats	Roasted Veggie Stuffed Pita	Apple-Cinnamon Wedge Bites	Cauliflower-Lentil Kofta
	3	Chickpea Frittata Squares	Lentil & Brown Rice Patties	Air-Fried Carrot Zucchini Chips	Spaghetti Squash Veggie Balls
	4	Cinnamon-Spiced Quinoa Cakes	Thai-Inspired Tofu Lettuce Boats	Curried Lentil Poppers	Butternut Chickpea Hash Stack
	5	Zucchini-Lentil Breakfast Hash	Air-Fried Mushroom-Spinach Rolls	Sweet Potato Toast Fingers	Eggplant-Millet Air Parm
	6	Plantain and Black Bean Nuggets	Sweet Potato Chickpea Pockets	Seasoned Green Pea Crunch	Moroccan-Spiced Carrot Patties
	7	Tofu-Turmeric Breakfast Cubes	Crispy Quinoa Salad Bites	Roasted Cauliflower Nuggets	Sweet Potato & Kale Air Casserole
Week 2:	8	Carrot Cake Baked Oat Squares	Zucchini-Carrot Fritter Sandwich	Crunchy Quinoa Clusters	Zucchini Lentil Lasagna Cups
	9	Apple-Cinnamon Breakfast Fries	Eggplant-Bulgur Medallions	Parsnip & Herb Wedges	Crunchy Quinoa-Stuffed Peppers
	10	Buckwheat & Date Mini Muffins	Tofu Kale Crunch Wrap	Plantain & Walnut Munchies	Broccoli-Cauliflower Curry Bites
	11	Avocado-Corn Breakfast Fritters	Smoky Black Bean Air Cakes	Tofu-Celery Air Sticks	Curried Rice and Chickpea Cakes
	12	Mango Millet Breakfast Bites	Roasted Red Pepper & Hummus Wrap	Sweet Date-Coconut Balls	Tofu-Pumpkin Rice Bake
	13	Cauliflower-Potato Morning Tots	Tomato-Lentil Crunch Sliders	Spicy Mushroom Snack Cubes	Mushroom-Stuffed Polenta Squares
	14	Air-Fried Berry Oat Clusters	Chickpea-Cauliflower Air Balls	Lemon-Garlic Broccoli Bites	Roasted Brussels Veggie Mix

Week	Day	Breakfast	Lunch	Snack or appetizer	Dinner
Week 3:	15	Roasted Brussels Veggie Mix	Broccoli-Sweet Potato Pocket	Beet Hummus Air-Fry Chips	Cabbage-Wrapped Spiced Lentils
	16	Crunchy Peanut Butter Oat Bites	Millet-Lime Veggie Boats	Ginger-Oat Mini Discs	Air-Fried Gnocchi with Herbs
	17	Golden Lentil Breakfast Bars	Crunchy Parsnip Wraps	Pumpkin-Crisp Snack Cakes	Crispy Eggplant and Corn Patties
	18	Savory Oat and Mushroom Balls	Carrot-Lentil Air Burgers	Maple Carrot Oat Crunch	Chickpea Mushroom Stroganoff Bites
	19	Air-Fried Polenta Slices	Cucumber Quinoa Salad Wrap	Seaweed & Rice Crumble Squares	Carrot-Zucchini Noodle Balls
	20	Sweet Beet & Walnut Crisps	Spicy Edamame Lettuce Cups	Crunchy Cucumber Tofu Rolls	Crunchy Black Bean Tofu Steaks
	21	Parsnip & Leek Hash Cups	Curried Chickpea Air Logs	Spiced Lentil Bites with Dill	Creamy Spinach Quinoa Cups
Week 4:	22	Quinoa-Pumpkin Mini Loaves	Green Bean & Rice Cakes	Banana-Almond Air Coins	Air-Fried Vegetable Tikka Parcels
	23	Green Pea and Herb Medallions	Herbed Zucchini Tofu Discs	Avocado & Quinoa Wafers	Sweet Corn & Leek Galettes
	24	Coconut-Chia Breakfast Rolls	BBQ Cauliflower Pita Pockets	Chickpea-Cranberry Crisps	Baked Turmeric Cauliflower Slabs
	25	Spiced Butternut Breakfast Fries	Garlic Sweet Corn Cakes	Jicama Lime Snack Cubes	Lentil-Rice Patties with Avocado Drizzle
	26	Air-Fried Apple Buckwheat Slices	Air-Fried Tempeh Veggie Skewers	Curry-Spiced Sweet Potato Slices	Tofu Stuffed Portobello Caps
	27	Tomato-Basil Breakfast Triangles	Roasted Root Veggie Samosas	Roasted Garlic Cauliflower Florets	Roasted Pepper Rice Cakes
	28	Millet-Cinnamon Crunch Wedges	Mushroom Brown Rice Nori Wraps	Sweet Date-Coconut Balls	Pumpkin-Spinach Air-Fry Casserole

Free Gift

Thank you! Discover your gift inside! Explore a diverse selection of DASH Diet for Beginners recipes for added inspiration. Gift it or share the PDF effortlessly with friends and family via a single click on WhatsApp or other social platforms. Bon appétit!

SCAN ME

Conclusion outline

Congratulations on completing The Plant-Based Air Fryer Cookbook for Beginners! By embarking on this journey, you've taken meaningful steps toward a healthier, more vibrant lifestyle while discovering how enjoyable and straightforward plant-based cooking can be. With the air fryer as your trusted kitchen companion, you've unlocked the ability to easily prepare flavorful, satisfying meals, reduce oil, cut down on cooking time, and preserve the natural goodness of whole foods.

The benefits of this lifestyle reach far beyond the dinner table. Choosing more plant-based options, you're supporting your long-term health, improving digestion, boosting energy levels, and contributing to better heart health and sustainable weight management. Additionally, you're playing a vital role in promoting environmental sustainability and reducing your ecological footprint. Through air frying, you also embrace a method that enhances the textures and flavors of plant-based ingredients while preserving their vital nutrients, making every meal as nourishing as it is delicious.

As you continue your culinary adventure, don't be afraid to experiment with new ingredients, seasonal produce, and creative flavor combinations. The recipes in this book are just the beginning. Use the skills and techniques you've learned to craft your own signature dishes, to bring variety and excitement to your kitchen every day. Remember, every slight, consistent change leads to lasting results, both for your personal well-being and for the planet.

Above all, approach this lifestyle with joy and a sense of curiosity. Every meal is a fresh opportunity to nourish your body, delight your taste buds, and make a positive impact in the world. May your air fryer continue to be a gateway to health, culinary creativity, and the simple pleasures of plant-based living.

Happy cooking, and here's to your continued success!

References

Academy of Nutrition and Dietetics. (2016). Position of the Academy of Nutrition and Dietetics: Vegetarian Diets. Journal of the Academy of Nutrition and Dietetics, 116(12), 1970–1980.

Harvard T.H. Chan School of Public Health. (n.d.). The Nutrition Source: Plant-Based Diets.

McDougall, J. (2012). The Starch Solution. Rodale Books.

Cleveland Clinic. (2021). The Health Benefits of Plant-Based Eating.

Mendez, L. (2019). Air Fryer Revolution: 100 Plant-Based Recipes for Guilt-Free Comfort Foods. Green Plate Press.

U.S. Department of Agriculture. (2020). Dietary Guidelines for Americans, 2020-2025.

Plant-Based Foods Association. (2022). Plant-Based Industry Annual Report.

Pollan, M. (2008). In Defense of Food: An Eater's Manifesto. Penguin Press.

Eshel, G., & Martin, P. A. (2006). Diet, Energy, and Global Warming. Earth Interactions, 10(9), 1–17.

American Heart Association. (2020). Plant-Based Diets: Are They Right for You?

Appendix 1: Measurement Conversion Chart

U.S. System	Metric
1 inch	2.54 centimeters
1 fluid ounce	29.57 milliliters
1 pint (16 ounces)	473.18 milliliters, 2 cups
1 quart (32 ounces)	1 liter, 4 cups
1 gallon (128 ounces)	4 liters, 16 cups
1 pound (16 ounces)	437.5 grams (0.4536 kilogram), 473.18 milliliters
1 ounces	2 tablespoons, 28 grams
1 cup (8 ounces)	237 milliliters
1 teaspoon	5 milliliters
1 tablespoon	15 milliliters (3 teaspoons)
Fahrenheit (subtract 32 and divide by 1.8 to get Celsius)	Centigrade (multiply by 1.8 and add 32 to get Fahrenheit)

Appendix 2: Index Recipes

A

Apple
Air-Fried Apple Buckwheat Slices - 27
Apple-Cinnamon Breakfast Fries - 18
Apple-Cinnamon Wedge Bites - 30
Apple-Raisin Oat Rounds - 83
Peanut Butter Apple Wedges - 77
Sweet Apple Lentil Muffins - 75

Avocado
Avocado & Quinoa Wafers - 41
Avocado-Corn Breakfast Fritters - 19
Lentil-Rice Patties with
Avocado Drizzle - 71
Chocolate Avocado Truffle Balls - 85

B

Banana
Air-Fried Banana Oat Patties - 15
Banana-Almond Air Coins - 40
Banana-Cocoa Mini Cakes - 80
Crispy Banana Oat Crumble - 75

Beet
Beet Hummus Air-Fry Chips - 37
Ginger Beet Cookie Slices - 83
Sweet Beet & Walnut Crisps - 24

Blueberry
Blueberry-Lime Crisp Cubes - 88

Broccoli
Broccoli-Cauliflower Curry Bites - 64
Broccoli-Chickpea Mini Cakes - 21
Broccoli-Sweet Potato Pocket - 52
Lemon-Garlic Broccoli Bites - 36

Buckwheat
Air-Fried Apple Buckwheat Slices - 27
Buckwheat & Date Mini Muffins - 19
Peach-Buckwheat Crisp - 86

Butternut Squash
Butternut Chickpea Hash Stack - 61
Spiced Butternut Breakfast Fries - 26

C

Cabbage
Cabbage-Wrapped Spiced Lentils - 66

Carrot
Carrot Cake Baked Oat Squares - 18
Carrot-Lentil Air Burgers - 53
Carrot-Zucchini Noodle Balls - 68
Cinnamon-Roasted Carrot Bars - 84
Maple Carrot Oat Crunch - 38
Moroccan-Spiced Carrot Patties - 62
Air-Fried Carrot Zucchini Chips - 30
Zucchini-Carrot Fritter Sandwich - 48
Coconut-Carrot Pudding Cups - 77

Cauliflower
Baked Turmeric Cauliflower Slabs - 71
BBQ Cauliflower Pita Pockets - 56
Cauliflower-Lentil Kofta - 59
Chickpea-Cauliflower Air Balls - 51
Roasted Garlic Cauliflower Florets - 43
Roasted Cauliflower Nuggets - 32
Broccoli-Cauliflower Curry Bites - 64

Chickpea
Chickpea Frittata Squares - 15
Chickpea-Cauliflower Air Balls - 51
Chickpea Mushroom Stroganoff Bites - 68
Chocolate Chickpea Crunch Bites - 76
Crispy Chickpea Snack Bombs - 29
Curried Chickpea Air Logs - 44
Sweet Potato Chickpea Pockets - 47
Broccoli-Chickpea Mini Cakes - 21
Chickpea-Cranberry Crisps - 41
Butternut Chickpea Hash Stack - 61
Curried Rice and Chickpea Cakes - 64

Coconut (shredded)
Coconut-Carrot Pudding Cups - 77
Coconut-Chia Breakfast Rolls - 26
Mango Coconut Rice Puffs - 80
Sweet Date-Coconut Balls - 35

Corn
Avocado-Corn Breakfast Fritters - 19

Corn & Black Bean Snack Balls - 33
Garlic Sweet Corn Cakes - 56
Sweet Corn & Leek Galettes - 70
Crispy Eggplant and Corn Patties - 67
Cucumber
Crunchy Cucumber Tofu Rolls - 39
Cucumber Quinoa Salad Wrap - 54

D

Date
Air-Fried Date-Nut Bars - 74
Orange-Date Bliss Squares - 81
Tahini-Date Energy Donuts - 85
Buckwheat & Date Mini Muffins - 19
Sweet Date-Coconut Balls - 35

E

Eggplant
Crispy Eggplant and Corn Patties - 67
Eggplant-Bulgur Medallions - 49
Eggplant-Millet Air Parm - 61

F

Figs
Stuffed Baked Figs with Walnuts - 82

G

Garlic
Garlic Sweet Corn Cakes - 56
Roasted Garlic Cauliflower Florets - 43
Lemon-Garlic Broccoli Bites - 36
Ginger
Ginger Beet Cookie Slices - 83
Ginger-Oat Mini Discs - 37
Green Bean
Green Bean & Rice Cakes - 55

J

Jicama
Jicama Lime Snack Cubes - 42

L

Lemon
Air-Fried Polenta Lemon Wedges - 86
Lemon-Garlic Broccoli Bites - 36
Lentil
Cauliflower-Lentil Kofta - 59
Curried Lentil Poppers - 31
Golden Lentil Breakfast Bars - 22
Sweet Apple Lentil Muffins - 75
Zucchini-Lentil Breakfast Hash - 16
Spiced Lentil Bites with Dill - 40
Lentil & Brown Rice Patties - 46
Tomato-Lentil Crunch Sliders - 51
Carrot-Lentil Air Burgers - 53
Zucchini Lentil Lasagna Cups - 63
Cabbage-Wrapped Spiced Lentils - 66
Lentil-Rice Patties with
Avocado Drizzle - 71

M

Millet
Eggplant-Millet Air Parm - 61
Mango Millet Breakfast Bites - 20
Millet-Cinnamon Crunch Wedges - 28
Millet-Lime Veggie Boats - 52
Vanilla Millet Pudding Puffs - 84
Mango
Mango Coconut Rice Puffs - 80
Mango Millet Breakfast Bites - 20
Mushroom
Air-Fried Mushroom-Spinach Rolls - 47
Chickpea Mushroom Stroganoff Bites - 68
Mushroom Brown Rice Nori Wraps - 58
Mushroom-Stuffed Polenta Squares - 65
Spicy Mushroom Snack Cubes - 36
Savory Oat and Mushroom Balls - 23

O

Oats
Air-Fried Banana Oat Patties - 15
Air-Fried Berry Oat Clusters - 21
Carrot Cake Baked Oat Squares - 18

Crunchy Peanut Butter Oat Bites - 22
Crispy Banana Oat Crumble - 75
Ginger-Oat Mini Discs - 37
Savory Oat and Mushroom Balls - 23
Maple Carrot Oat Crunch - 38
Air-Fried Berry-Filled Oat Discs - 78
Apricot-Oat Tartlets - 82
Apple-Raisin Oat Rounds - 83
Roasted Strawberry Oat Fritters - 87

P

Parsnip
Parsnip & Herb Wedges - 34
Parsnip & Leek Hash Cups - 24
Crunchy Parsnip Wraps - 53
Peach
Peach-Buckwheat Crisp - 86
Peanut Butter
Crunchy Peanut Butter Oat Bites - 22
Peanut Butter Apple Wedges - 77
Pineapple
Pineapple Basil Dessert Skewers - 87
Plantain
Plantain and Black Bean Nuggets - 17
Plantain & Walnut Munchies - 34
Polenta (coarse cornmeal)
Air-Fried Polenta Lemon Wedges - 86
Air-Fried Polenta Slices - 23
Mushroom-Stuffed Polenta Squares - 65
Pumpkin
Pumpkin-Chia Spice Cookies - 79
Pumpkin-Crisp Snack Cakes - 38
Pumpkin-Spinach Air-Fry Casserole - 73
Quinoa-Pumpkin Mini Loaves - 25
Tofu-Pumpkin Rice Bake - 65

Q

Quinoa
Baked Cinnamon Quinoa Squares - 76
Cinnamon-Spiced Quinoa Cakes - 16
Creamy Spinach Quinoa Cups - 69
Crunchy Quinoa Clusters - 33

Crispy Quinoa Salad Bites - 48
Cucumber Quinoa Salad Wrap - 54
Quinoa-Pumpkin Mini Loaves - 25
Crunchy Quinoa Clusters - 33
Avocado & Quinoa Wafers - 41
Crunchy Quinoa-Stuffed Peppers - 63

R

Rice
Curried Rice and Chickpea Cakes - 64
Green Bean & Rice Cakes - 55
Mango Coconut Rice Puffs - 80
Mushroom Brown Rice Nori Wraps - 58
Roasted Pepper Rice Cakes - 72
Seaweed & Rice Crumble Squares - 39
Lentil & Brown Rice Patties - 46
Tofu-Pumpkin Rice Bake - 65
Lentil-Rice Patties with
Avocado Drizzle - 71

S

Seaweed
Seaweed & Rice Crumble Squares - 39
Spinach
Air-Fried Mushroom-Spinach Rolls - 47
Creamy Spinach Quinoa Cups - 69
Pumpkin-Spinach Air-Fry Casserole - 73
Squash
Spaghetti Squash Veggie Balls - 60
Strawberry
Roasted Strawberry Oat Fritters - 87
Sweet Potato
Maple-Glazed Sweet Potato Coins - 79
Sweet Potato & Kale Air Casserole - 62
Sweet Potato Breakfast Boats - 14
Sweet Potato Chickpea Pockets - 47
Sweet Potato Toast Fingers - 31
Curry-Spiced Sweet Potato Slices - 42

T

Tahini
Tahini-Date Energy Donuts - 85

Tofu
Air-Fried Tofu Steak with Chimichurri - 60
Crunchy Black Bean Tofu Steaks - 69
Herbed Zucchini Tofu Discs - 55
Tofu-Celery Air Sticks - 35
Tofu Kale Crunch Wrap - 49
Tofu-Pumpkin Rice Bake - 65
Tofu Stuffed Portobello Caps - 72
Tofu-Turmeric Breakfast Cubes - 17
Crunchy Cucumber Tofu Rolls - 39
Thai-Inspired Tofu Lettuce Boats - 46

Tomato
Tomato-Basil Breakfast Triangles - 27
Tomato-Lentil Crunch Sliders - 51

V

Vanilla
Vanilla Millet Pudding Puffs - 84

W

Walnuts
Plantain & Walnut Munchies - 34
Stuffed Baked Figs with Walnuts - 82
Sweet Beet & Walnut Crisps - 24

Z

Zucchini
Air-Fried Carrot Zucchini Chips - 30
Carrot-Zucchini Noodle Balls - 68
Herbed Zucchini Tofu Discs - 55
Zucchini-Carrot Fritter Sandwich - 48
Zucchini Lentil Lasagna Cups - 63
Zucchini-Lentil Breakfast Hash - 16

Notes

Notes